YOUR recipe could appear in our next cookbook!

Share your tried & true family favorites with us instantly at
www.gooseberrypatch.com
If you'd rather jot 'em down by hand, just mail this form to...
Gooseberry Patch • Cookbooks – Call for Recipes
PO Box 812 • Columbus, OH 43216-0812

If your recipe is selected for a book, you'll receive a FREE copy!

Please share only your original recipes or those that you have made your own over the years.

Recipe Name:

Number of Servings:

Any fond memories about this recipe? Special touches you like to add
or handy shortcuts?

Ingredients (include specific measurements):

Instructions (continue on back if needed):

Special Code: **cookbookspage**

Over ➤

Extra space for recipe if needed:

Tell us about yourself...

Your complete contact information is needed so that we can send you your FREE cookbook, if your recipe is published. Phone numbers and email addresses are kept private and will only be used if we have questions about your recipe.

Name:

Address:

City: State: Zip:

Email:

Daytime Phone:

Thank you! Vickie & JoAnn

Gooseberry Patch

Mom's GO-TO RECIPES

Feed your family well with quick, comforting meals that are always a hit

Gooseberry Patch

An imprint of Globe Pequot
64 South Main Street
Essex, CT 06426

www.gooseberrypatch.com

1•800•854•6673

Copyright 2022, Gooseberry Patch 978-1-62093-497-5
Photo Edition is a major revision of **Mom's Go-To Recipes**.

Do you have a tried & true recipe...

tip, craft or memory that you'd like to see featured in
a **Gooseberry Patch** cookbook? Visit our website at
www.gooseberrypatch.com and follow the
easy steps to submit your favorite family recipe.

Or send them to us at:

Gooseberry Patch
PO Box 812
Columbus, OH 43216-0812

Don't forget to include the number of servings your recipe makes,
plus your name, address, phone number and email address. If we
select your recipe, your name will appear right along with it...
and you'll receive a **FREE** copy of the book!

Contents

Dedication

To everyone who knows that there's nothing better than Mom's good home cooking, served up with love!

Appreciation

To all of you who shared your best, tried & true favorites for family meals together.

Off You Go!
BREAKFASTS

Mom's GO-TO *Recipes*

Breakfast BLT & Egg Sandwiches

Jill Ball
Highland, UT

I am always looking for new breakfast ideas for my family that will stick with them during school. This is a winner...easy, different and delicious! These can even be wrapped in a paper towel and eaten on the go. It's very easy to scale down for fewer sandwiches.

12 slices whole-wheat or
   white bread
1 lb. thin-sliced bacon
1 to 2 T. butter
1 doz. eggs, lightly beaten

salt and pepper to taste
light mayonnaise to taste
Garnish: sliced tomatoes,
   lettuce leaves

Toast bread and set aside. In a large skillet, cook bacon until crisp; drain on paper towels. Meanwhile, melt butter in a separate large skillet. Add eggs and scramble until cooked through; season with salt and pepper. For each sandwich, spread 2 slices of toasted bread with mayonnaise. Layer one slice of toast with a spoonful of eggs, 2 tomato slices, 2 to 3 bacon slices and lettuce. Add the second slice of toast on top. Slice and serve. Makes 6 sandwiches.

Everyone loves crispy bacon! Here's the easiest way to make a panful. Arrange bacon slices on a wire rack set in a rimmed baking sheet... toss on a few extra slices for your next BLT! Bake at 450 degrees for 15 to 20 minutes, to desired crispness.

Off You Go!
BREAKFASTS

Speedy Egg Sandwiches

Penny Sherman
Ava, MO

My kids loved those breakfast sandwiches from the fast-food drive-through, but I knew I could make them better at home. They like these sandwiches just as much! Sometimes I'll add a heat & serve sausage patty for a heartier breakfast.

2 eggs, beaten
salt and pepper to taste
2 English muffins, split and
    toasted

softened butter to taste
2 slices Cheddar cheese
2 slices tomato

In a bowl, whisk together eggs, salt and pepper. Divide egg mixture between 2 well-greased microwave-safe mugs. Microwave on high, one mug at a time, until eggs are puffed and set, 30 to 45 seconds. To serve, spread toasted English muffins with butter; fill each muffin with cooked egg, a cheese slice and a tomato slice. Serve immediately. Makes 2 sandwiches.

A fresh, fun side for breakfast...fruit kabobs! Just slide juicy strawberries, banana chunks, kiwi slices and orange wedges onto wooden skewers. Serve with vanilla yogurt for dipping, if you like.

Mom's GO-TO *Recipes*

Freezer French Toast Sticks

Melanie Lowe
Dover, DE

These are a favorite of my little girls! I'm happy to make them because they're so easy to fix. I serve the syrup or jam alongside in a little cup for dipping.

8 slices thick-cut Texas toast,
   crusts trimmed if desired
3 eggs, beaten
1-1/2 c. milk
1 t. cinnamon
2 T. sugar
2 t. vanilla extract
Garnish: maple syrup,
   fruit preserves

Cut each slice of toast into 3 strips; set aside. In a large shallow bowl, whisk together remaining ingredients except garnish. Line a baking sheet with aluminum foil; spray with non-stick vegetable spray. Dip each piece of toast into egg mixture, coating it on all sides; shake off the excess and place on baking sheet. Bake at 350 degrees for 12 minutes; turn over strips and spray lightly with vegetable spray. Bake for another 12 to 15 minutes, until golden and cooked through. Serve warm, garnished as desired, or freeze. Serves 4 to 6.

To freeze: Bake as above; cool completely and freeze on a tray. Transfer strips to a plastic freezer bag. To serve, microwave for 30 to 60 seconds, until warmed through.

For a scrumptious pancake and waffle topping, combine 1/2 cup fresh blueberries, 1/2 cup softened butter and one tablespoon honey in a blender. Process until smooth. Yum!

Off You Go!
BREAKFASTS

Silver Dollar Pancakes

*Geneva Rogers
Gillette, WY*

*My grandkids love these little pancakes, even though
they don't know what a silver dollar is!*

2 eggs, beaten
1 c. milk

2 c. biscuit baking mix
Garnish: butter, maple syrup

In a large bowl, combine eggs, milk and biscuit mix. Whisk together,
just until well moistened. Drop batter by tablespoonfuls onto a greased
hot griddle. Cook until pancakes begin to bubble and edges are slightly
dry. Flip over; cook until golden. Serve with butter and maple syrup.
Makes 4 servings.

Berry Pancake Topping

*Barb Bargdill
Gooseberry Patch*

A dollop of this sweet topping makes any waffle or pancake special.

3 c. assorted berries,
   fresh or frozen

3 T. sugar
2 t. cornstarch

Combine all ingredients in a large microwave-safe bowl; toss until well
mixed. Microwave on high for 2 minutes; stir. Continue to microwave
for 2 to 3-1/2 minutes, until steamy and slightly thickened. Serve
immediately, or cover and refrigerate up to 3 days. Makes 8 servings.

Easiest kiddie breakfast treat ever! Spread a hot dog bun with
peanut butter and pop in a ripe banana. Add a few mini chocolate
chips for a treat...just fold and eat!

Mom's GO-TO *Recipes*

Sunrise Skillet

Melody Taynor
Everett, WA

*When our kids want to camp out in the backyard, I just
have to wake them to the aroma of a delicious breakfast...
and this recipe does the trick every time.*

1/2 lb. bacon	6 eggs, beaten
4 c. potatoes, peeled and cubed	1 c. shredded Cheddar cheese
1/2 onion, chopped	Optional: chopped green onions

Cook bacon in a cast-iron skillet over the slow-burning coals of a
campfire or on a stove over medium heat until crisply cooked. Remove
bacon from skillet; set aside. Stir potatoes and onion into drippings.
Cover and cook until potatoes are tender, about 10 to 12 minutes.
Crumble bacon into potatoes. Stir in eggs; cover and cook until set,
about 2 minutes. Sprinkle with cheese and onions, if desired; let stand
until cheese melts. Serves 6 to 8.

Shopping for oranges or grapefruits for breakfast?
Choose the heaviest ones of their size...you'll find
they are the juiciest.

Off You Go!
BREAKFASTS

Eggs in Bacon Rings

Janis Parr
Ontario, Canada

These neat little breakfast cups are tasty, nutritious and portable.
Our kids love to grab one to eat on the run on those busy mornings
when a sit-down breakfast just isn't possible.

6 slices bread, toasted and
    buttered
6 slices bacon

6 eggs
salt and pepper to taste

Grease 6 custard cups or muffin cups. With a cookie cutter, cut out a
circle from each slice of toast to fit the bottoms of cups; add to cups and
set aside. Place bacon slices on a microwave-safe plate; cover with a
paper towel and microwave for 4 to 6 minutes, until cooked but not
crisp. Drain on paper towels; wrap a bacon slice around the inside of
each muffin cup. Break an egg into each bacon ring; season with salt
and pepper. Bake at 350 degrees for 6 to 7 minutes, until eggs are set
as desired. Serves 6.

Turkey Bacon Biscuits

Jessica Delia
Preble, NY

One of our children has Crohn's disease and can't eat a lot of foods.
I modified a recipe I'd found to fit our family.

16-oz. tube refrigerated jumbo
    flaky biscuits
1 lb. turkey bacon, chopped
1 t. Dijon mustard

8-oz. pkg. Cheddar cheese, cubed
1/4 to 1/2 c. mayonnaise,
    divided

Spray 8 large muffin cups with non-stick vegetable spray. Press a
biscuit into each cup to form a basket; set aside. In a food processor,
combine uncooked bacon, mustard, cheese and 1/4 cup mayonnaise.
Process until coarsely chopped; add remaining mayonnaise, if too dry.
Scoop mixture into biscuit baskets. Bake at 350 degrees for 20 minutes,
or until biscuits are golden and bacon is crisp. Makes 8 servings.

Mom's GO-TO *Recipes*

Berry Good Whole-Grain Waffles

Marian Buckley
Fontana, CA

Whole-wheat flour and wheat germ make these yummy waffles nutritious. Fresh berries make them delicious!

1-1/2 c. whole-wheat flour
2 T. toasted wheat germ
2 T. sugar
1-1/2 t. baking powder
1/2 t. salt
1 egg, beaten
1-1/2 c. milk

1/4 c. canola oil
1 t. vanilla extract
Garnish: maple syrup,
    blueberries or sliced
    strawberries, sweetened
    plain Greek yogurt

In a large bowl, whisk together flour, wheat germ, sugar, baking powder and salt. In another bowl, whisk together egg, milk, oil and vanilla. Add egg mixture to flour mixture; stir until just combined. Add batter by 1/2 cupfuls to a preheated greased waffle iron. Cook according to manufacturer's instructions. Garnish as desired. Serves 4.

Tempt fussy kids with grilled cheese sandwiches for breakfast. Grilled peanut butter sammies are tasty too. Toast the sandwiches on a waffle iron instead of a griddle...kids will love 'em!

12

Off You Go! BREAKFASTS

Apple Pancakes

Nicole Chapman
Tampa, FL

A healthy way to start your day, any time of year! I like to make this for my kids...even my picky child who doesn't like a lot of things will eat these. They freeze well, so I freeze leftover pancakes on a baking sheet and bag them for another day. My kids like to toast them in the toaster.

2 c. pancake mix
1/2 c. quick-cooking oats,
   uncooked
1 c. milk
1 c. water

1/4 c. butter, melted
2 t. cinnamon
1 c. apple, peeled, cored and
   finely grated

In a large bowl, combine all ingredients except apple. Beat until smooth; fold in apple. Scoop batter by 1/4 cupfuls onto a hot buttered griddle, spreading to 3-1/2 inches each. Cook over medium heat for 2 to 3 minutes, until bubbly and edges of pancakes are dry. With a wide spatula, turn; cook for 2 minutes more, or until golden. Makes 8 to 12 pancakes.

Keep a tin of apple pie spice on hand to jazz up pancakes, muffins and coffee cakes...a quick shake adds cinnamon, nutmeg and allspice all at once.

Mom's GO-TO *Recipes*

Monkey Bread

Rebecca Ivey
Lagrange, GA

I first tried this recipe one year for a Christmas breakfast, and it was an instant hit! It's much too tasty to have just once a year.

1/2 c. butter, sliced
1 c. brown sugar, packed
1 c. sugar
1-1/2 T. cinnamon

4 7-1/2 oz. tubes refrigerated
   biscuits, quartered
Optional: 1/2 c. raisins, chopped
   pecans or flaked coconut

In a saucepan over medium heat, bring butter and brown sugar to a boil. Stir until brown sugar is dissolved; cool for 10 minutes. Meanwhile, combine sugar and cinnamon in a plastic zipping bag; mix well. Add biscuit pieces, a few at a time; shake to coat well. Arrange biscuit pieces in a buttered Bundt® pan, drizzling some of brown sugar mixture over each layer. Sprinkle layers with nuts, raisins or coconut, if desired. Bake at 350 degrees for 45 minutes. Allow to cool 15 minutes before removing from pan. Turn upside-down onto a plate and serve warm. Serves 8.

Cowboy Coffee Cake

Ann Christie
Glasgow, KY

Our family loved to have this coffee cake for breakfast on Sunday mornings before church. It's a yummy treat to fix quickly.

2 11-oz. tubes refrigerated
   biscuits
1/4 c. butter, melted
1/3 c. brown sugar, packed

1/3 c. chopped pecans
1 t. cinnamon
Optional: 3/4 c. powdered sugar,
   1 T. milk

Arrange biscuits in a lightly greased 9" round pan, overlapping edges. Combine all except optional ingredients; spread evenly over biscuits. Bake at 350 degrees for 22 minutes, or until golden. If desired, whisk together powdered sugar and milk; drizzle over top. Serve warm. Serves 6.

Off You Go!
BREAKFASTS

Yummy Frozen Fruit Salad Cups *Paula Ramsay*
Ashville, OH

*This is a recipe I like to make for holidays year 'round! I love
the combo of the pineapple, strawberries and bananas...
so refreshing! Feel free to substitute any fruits you prefer.*

1/2 c. water	10-oz. pkg. frozen strawberries,
3/4 c. sugar	thawed
4 ripe bananas, sliced	2 c. apricot nectar
15-1/4 oz. can crushed pineapple	1/8 t. salt
in juice	

In a small saucepan over medium-high heat, bring water and sugar
to a boil. Reduce heat to medium-low. Simmer until syrupy, 8 to
10 minutes; cool. Combine remaining ingredients in a large bowl; do
not drain fruits. Stir in cooled syrup. Spoon fruit mixture into 18 silicone
or aluminum baking cups. Freeze until firm, at least 6 hours. Let stand
at room temperature for 5 minutes before serving. Makes 1-1/2 dozen.

Come along inside...we'll see if tea and buns can make
the world a better place.
– Kenneth Grahame

Freezer Breakfast Burritos

Nichole Sullivan
Santa Fe, TX

A great on-the-go breakfast for kids and adults alike! I use my own garden-fresh homemade salsa, but your favorite store-bought salsa is fine too. Add some sautéed peppers and onions, if you like.

1 lb. ground pork breakfast
    sausage
1 doz. eggs, beaten
2 T. butter
salt and pepper to taste

1/4 c. favorite salsa
24 burrito-size flour tortillas
8-oz. pkg. shredded Cheddar
    cheese

Brown sausage in a skillet over medium heat; drain and set aside. In a separate large skillet, scramble eggs in butter over medium-low heat. Season with salt and pepper. Add sausage and salsa to eggs; stir well. Add a spoonful of egg mixture to each tortilla; top with cheese. Roll up burrito-style, folding in 2 sides and rolling up. Serve immediately, or freeze. Makes 2 dozen.

To freeze: Prepare as above. Layer burritos on a baking sheet, seam-side down; freeze completely. Wrap burritos in plastic wrap, individually or in pairs; freeze in plastic freezer bags. To serve, microwave for 2 to 3 minutes, until warmed through.

A buttery slice of cinnamon toast warms you right up on a chilly morning. Spread softened butter generously on one side of toasted white bread and sprinkle with cinnamon-sugar. Broil for one to 2 minutes, until hot and bubbly.

Off You Go!
BREAKFASTS

Break-of-Day Breakfast Pizza

Tracie Spencer
Rogers, KY

Love this recipe because it's something different for breakfast!
Add some mushrooms and black olives too.

1 lb. ground pork sausage
8-oz. tube refrigerated
   crescent rolls
8-oz. pkg. pizza-blend cheese
6 eggs, beaten

1/2 c. milk
3/4 t. dried oregano
1/8 t. pepper
Optional: finely diced green
   and red peppers

Cook sausage in a skillet over medium heat until browned; drain and set aside. Separate crescent dough into 8 triangles. In a greased 12" pizza pan or 13"x9" baking sheet, arrange triangles with elongated points toward the center, forming a circle. Press together perforations; turn up sides to form a crust. Bake on lower oven rack at 375 degrees for 5 minutes, or until crust is puffy. Remove from oven; reduce oven temperature to 350 degrees. Spoon sausage over dough; sprinkle with cheese. Whisk together eggs, milk and seasonings; pour over top. Return to lower rack; bake at 350 degrees for 30 to 35 minutes, until cheese is melted. Garnish with green and red peppers, if desired. Makes 6 to 8 servings.

Keep hard-boiled eggs on hand for speedy breakfast snacks,
salad toppers and nutritious snacks. Here's a tip...if you boil
eggs that have been refrigerated at least 7 to 10 days,
the shells will slip right off.

Mom's GO-TO Recipes

Ham & Cheese Bake

Elizabeth Smithson
Mayfield, KY

An easy family favorite! When my kids were home, the boys loved breakfast the best. I always tried to please them...this did!

8-oz. pkg. shredded mozzarella
   cheese
1/2 c. cooked ham, diced
5 eggs, beaten

3/4 c. milk
1/4 t. dried basil
salt and pepper to taste

Layer cheese and ham in a greased 9" pie plate; set aside. In a bowl, whisk together eggs, milk and seasonings; pour into pie plate. Bake at 350 degrees for 30 to 35 minutes. Let stand for 10 minutes before cutting into wedges. Serves 6 to 8.

Sausage & Cheese Muffins

Jennifer Dorward
Jefferson, GA

My mom got this recipe from a lady she used to work with. We have enjoyed it so much! We used to save these muffins for special occasions like holiday mornings, but they're just so yummy that I make them all the time now. It's great to make a big batch over the weekend, and then heat & eat on busy weekday mornings.

16-oz. pkg. ground pork
   breakfast sausage
10-3/4 oz. can Cheddar cheese
   soup

1/2 c. milk
2-1/2 c. biscuit baking mix
1 c. shredded Cheddar cheese

Brown sausage in a skillet over medium heat; drain and cool. Combine sausage with remaining ingredients; stir just until combined. Spoon mixture into greased muffin cups. Bake at 375 degrees for 15 minutes, or until golden. Makes 12 to 16.

For the fluffiest scrambled eggs ever, here's a secret...stir in a pinch of baking powder!

Off You Go!
BREAKFASTS

Pancake Jelly Sandwiches

Mel Chencharick
Julian, PA

If you don't care for syrup on your pancakes, you'll like these.
They're great to eat on the go...kids will love them!

2 c. biscuit baking mix
1 t. cinnamon
1/4 t. salt
1 c. milk

2 eggs, lightly beaten
Garnish: fruit preserves,
  jam or jelly
Optional: peanut butter

In a large bowl, combine biscuit mix, cinnamon and salt. Stir in milk
and eggs until blended. Pour batter by 1/4 cupfuls onto a greased hot
griddle; turn when bubbles form on top. Cook until golden on the other
side. Spread half of the pancakes with jam and peanut butter, if desired;
top with remaining pancakes. Makes 5 servings.

Is a loaf of bread too large for your family? As soon as you
bring home a fresh loaf, wrap half in plastic wrap and freeze.
It'll keep its fresh-baked taste for 2 to 3 months...just thaw at room
temperature. Or pop still-frozen slices directly into the toaster.

Mom's GO-TO *Recipes*

Peachy Baked Oatmeal

Hannah Hilgendorf
Nashotah, WI

*This is a nourishing, stick-to-your-ribs breakfast. It can be made
ahead and baked in the morning, or prepared, baked and
warmed up later to serve. Children and adults love it!*

2 eggs, beaten
1/2 c. brown sugar, packed
1-1/2 t. baking powder
1/4 t. salt
1-1/2 t. cinnamon
1/2 t. nutmeg
1-1/2 t. vanilla extract

3/4 c. milk
3 c. long-cooking oats, uncooked
1/3 c. oil
16-oz. can sliced peaches,
  partially drained
Garnish: warm milk

In a bowl, combine eggs, brown sugar, baking powder, salt, spices
and vanilla; beat well. Add remaining ingredients except garnish;
mix thoroughly. Spoon into a greased 8"x8" baking pan. Bake at
375 degrees for 20 to 25 minutes, until center is set. Serve in bowls,
topped with warm milk. Serves 6.

Make mini portions of baked oatmeal. Just spoon the oatmeal
mixture into a muffin tin lined with paper muffin cups and bake.
Any leftovers can be frozen for another meal.

Off You Go! BREAKFASTS

Doug's Favorite Granola

*Janet Sharp
Milford, OH*

This granola is a favorite breakfast meal for my husband, especially on busy mornings. I make it ahead of time and store it in a covered container in the refrigerator. Then for a hearty, healthy breakfast, just top with milk in a bowl. It is delicious and can be also served as a topping for yogurt or ice cream, or enjoyed as a tasty snack.

3 c. old-fashioned oats,
   uncooked
1/2 c. chopped walnuts
1/2 c. chopped almonds
1/2 c. chopped pecans

Optional: 1/2 c. raisins
1/2 c. pure maple syrup
1/2 t. cinnamon
1/4 t. salt

Combine all ingredients in a large bowl. Mix well to coat everything with syrup. Spread mixture on a large baking sheet coated with non-stick vegetable spray. Bake at 300 degrees for about 30 minutes, until golden, stirring occasionally. Place baking sheet on a wire rack; let cool completely. Transfer to an airtight container; keep refrigerated up to 2 weeks. Makes 9 servings.

Half-pint Mason jars are just right for filling with layers of fresh fruit, creamy yogurt and crunchy granola. They can even be popped into the fridge the night before, then topped with granola just before serving. Add a spoon and breakfast is served!

Chocolate-Banana Breakfast Bars *Lisa Ashton*
Aston, PA

*When I taste-tested these bars on my daughter as a dessert,
she said they were filling enough to be eaten for breakfast!*

2 ripe bananas, mashed
1/2 c. brown sugar, packed
1/4 c. sugar
1/4 c. butter, softened
1 t. vanilla extract
1 egg, beaten

1 c. all-purpose flour
2 c. rolled oats, uncooked
1 t. baking soda
1/4 t. salt
3/4 c. semi-sweet chocolate chips

In a large bowl, combine bananas, sugars, butter and vanilla; beat well.
Add egg; mix thoroughly and set aside. In another bowl, combine flour,
oats, baking soda and salt. Add to banana mixture and mix well. Fold in
chocolate chips. Spread mixture in a 13"x9" baking pan coated with
non-stick vegetable spray. Bake at 350 degrees for 22 to 25 minutes,
until a knife inserted in the center comes out clean. Cool completely;
cut into bars. Wrap individually in plastic wrap. Makes 16 bars.

Make breakfast bars extra special! Wrap each one in a strip of
colorful paper and tie with a ribbon. So pretty on a buffet tray...
or a welcome surprise in a lunchbox.

Off You Go!
BREAKFASTS

Cranberry Upside-Down Muffins

Barbara Girlardo
Pittsburgh, PA

We love making these muffins on Sunday mornings.
The Cranberry Topping makes them even more delightful!

2-1/2 c. all-purpose flour
1/2 c. sugar
1 T. baking powder
1/2 t. salt

1-1/4 c. milk
1/3 c. butter, melted and
  slightly cooled
1 egg, beaten

Combine flour, sugar, baking powder and salt in a large bowl; blend well. Add milk, butter and egg to flour mixture; stir just until moistened. Spoon Cranberry Topping into 18 greased muffin cups. Spoon batter over topping, filling each cup 2/3 full. Bake at 400 degrees for 16 to 18 minutes, until a toothpick inserted in center comes out clean. Immediately invert onto a wire rack placed on wax paper; serve warm. Makes 1-1/2 dozen.

Cranberry Topping:

1/2 c. cranberries, halved
1/2 c. chopped nuts
1/3 c. brown sugar, packed

1/4 c. butter
1/2 t. cinnamon

Combine all ingredients in a small saucepan. Cook over medium heat until brown sugar dissolves. Cool 10 minutes.

Enjoy a warm muffin anytime! Wrap extra muffins in aluminum foil and keep frozen up to a month. To serve, reheat at 300 degrees for 15 to 18 minutes.

Mom's GO-TO Recipes

Choco-Milk

Juana Rodriguez
American Falls, ID

I grew up in Mexico with this breakfast shake that my mom used to make to stretch the small amount of milk she could afford for her five kids. I have added a few ingredients to make it even better...now it's one of my kids' favorites. We actually enjoy it any time of day!

1/2 ripe banana, sliced
6 strawberries, hulled
2 c. skim or low-fat milk
1/4 c. vanilla yogurt

3 T. chocolate or strawberry
   drink mix
1/2 t. cinnamon
Garnish: cinnamon-sugar

In a blender, combine all ingredients except garnish. Process on high speed until smooth. If a sweeter taste is desired, add a little more drink mix and blend to combine. Pour into 2 tall glasses; sprinkle with cinnamon-sugar and serve. Makes 2 servings.

Mom's Best Fruit Smoothies

April Haury
Paramus, NJ

This simple smoothie is one of our family favorites...and so easy!

1-1/2 c. fresh or frozen peaches,
   cut into chunks
2 mangoes, pitted and diced
1 banana, cut into chunks

8-oz. container non-fat
   plain yogurt
1 T. honey

Combine fruit and yogurt in a blender. Process until smooth; pour into tall glasses. Makes 3 servings.

Just a Bite
FOR LUNCH

Mom's GO-TO Recipes

Pizzeria Soup

Janis Parr
Ontario, Canada

This is a delicious soup...and it's so simple to make.

1 T. oil
1/2 c. onion, chopped
1/2 c. sliced mushrooms
1/4 c. green pepper, diced
28-oz. can stewed tomatoes

1 c. beef broth
1 c. thinly sliced pepperoni
1/4 t. dried oregano
Garnish: shredded mozzarella
 cheese

Heat oil in a large soup pot over medium heat; add onion, mushrooms and green pepper. Cook for 2 minutes, or until soft. Cut up tomatoes; add to the pot along with their juice. Add broth, pepperoni and oregano; stir well. Bring to a boil; reduce heat to low and simmer for about 15 minutes. Ladle into bowls; sprinkle each bowl with cheese. Serves 4.

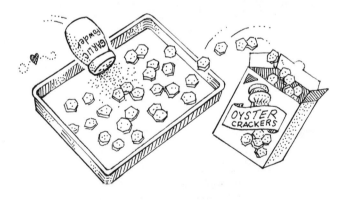

Crisp, savory crackers make any bowl of soup even tastier!
To 1-1/2 cups oyster crackers, add 1-1/2 tablespoons melted butter, 1/4 teaspoon dried thyme and 1/4 teaspoon garlic powder. Mix well and spread on a baking sheet. Bake at 350 degrees for 10 minutes, or until crunchy and golden.

Ratatouille Soup

Diana Chaney
Olathe, KS

Thanks to the movies, even little kids know about ratatouille, a tasty combo of eggplant and other veggies. Sometimes I'll swap out the macaroni for alphabet pasta, just to tickle the kids.

1 lb. ground beef
24-oz. jar tomato-basil
    pasta sauce
10-1/2 oz. can beef broth
2 c. water
3-1/2 c. eggplant, peeled
    and cubed

1-1/2 c. zucchini, peeled
    and cubed
1 c. green, red and/or yellow
    pepper, chopped
1 c. elbow macaroni, uncooked
Optional: shredded Parmesan
    cheese

Brown beef in a soup pot over medium heat; drain. Stir in remaining ingredients except macaroni and optional cheese. Bring to a boil over medium-high heat; reduce heat to low. Cover and cook for 15 minutes, stirring once or twice. Return heat to medium; stir in macaroni. Cook for 10 minutes or until macaroni is tender, stirring occasionally. Serve topped with cheese, if desired. Serves 4 to 6.

Tom's Grilled Swiss-Colby Sandwich

Thomas Hiegel
Union City, OH

This is the best-tasting grilled cheese sandwich I've ever come up with, and it's so easy to fix. Swiss-Colby cheese is hard to find, but worth looking for.

2 slices soft whole-grain bread
1 slice Swiss-Colby cheese

1 slice Colby cheese
2 T. butter, softened

Make a sandwich with one bread slice, both cheese slices and remaining bread slice. Spread butter over outside of sandwich. Add sandwich to a non-stick skillet over medium-high heat. Toast on both sides until golden and cheese is melted. Serve warm. Makes one sandwich.

Mom's GO-TO *Recipes*

Yummy Easy Corn Chowder

Kathy Courington
Canton, GA

The first time I tasted this soup, I thought, "Wow, is this good!"
Our pastor's wife said at the time that it was easy to make
too. She was kind enough to give me the recipe.

16-oz. pkg. reduced-fat ground
    pork sausage
1 c. onion, chopped
12-oz. can evaporated milk
1 c. skim or 2% milk

1 c. water
15-oz. can corn
14-3/4 oz. can creamed corn
1 russet potato, peeled and diced
salt and pepper to taste

In a large skillet over medium heat, cook sausage and onion until
sausage is browned; drain. Stir in milks and water; bring to a boil. Add
both cans of corn, potato and seasonings. Reduce heat to medium-low
and simmer for 1-1/2 to 2 hours, stirring occasionally. If too thick, stir
in a little more milk or water. Makes 6 to 8 servings.

Mom's best advice for success in the kitchen...read through the recipe
first! Make sure you have all the ingredients, equipment and time
needed to make the recipe. You'll be glad you did!

Just a Bite FOR LUNCH

Chicken & Wild Rice Soup

Marian Forck
Chamois, MO

When I was little, my mother always made soup for me. She said it would make me feel better, and she was right! If you prefer white rice, there's no need to soak...just prepare according to the package.

1 c. wild rice, uncooked
2 c. water, divided
8 T. butter, divided
2 boneless, skinless chicken
    breasts, cubed
1 c. carrots, peeled and
    thinly sliced

1 onion, diced
1/2 c. celery, chopped
2 10-3/4 oz. cans cream of
    chicken soup
2-2/3 c. milk
3 T. sliced almonds
1-1/2 T. dried parsley

In a bowl, cover rice with one cup water. Let soak for 6 to 8 hours or overnight; drain. Bring remaining water to a boil in a small pan over medium-high heat. Stir in drained rice. Boil until water level dips below rice, about 10 minutes; remove from heat. In a large saucepan, melt 2 tablespoons butter over medium heat. Add chicken, carrots, onion and celery; cook for 15 minutes. Transfer chicken mixture to a large soup pot; stir in soup, milk, almonds, parsley and remaining butter. Bring to a boil, stirring constantly. Reduce heat to low and stir in cooked rice. Simmer, uncovered, for 15 minutes, stirring occasionally and adding more water or milk to thin, if needed. Makes 6 to 8 servings.

Oversized glass jars make convenient canisters for storing dried beans, rice and pasta...no more messy half-used packages in the cupboard! Customize them with vinyl stick-on letters for your favorite pantry items.

Mom's GO-TO Recipes

Chicken Caesar Salad Wrap

Courtney Stultz
Weir, KS

This wrap is very simple to make and full of flavor! Wraps are one of our go-to quick lunch options and we always have shredded chicken on hand to make it easier.

1 c. cooked chicken breast, shredded
2 T. Caesar salad dressing
1/4 c. cherry tomatoes, diced
1/2 c. salad greens, finely chopped
1/4 c. shredded Parmesan cheese
4 tortilla shells, sandwich wraps or lettuce leaves

In a bowl, combine chicken, dressing, tomatoes, greens and cheese. Toss until combined. Spoon 1/4 cup of mixture into the center of each shell, wrap or leaf; roll up and serve. Makes 4 servings.

Tangy Tuna Melt

Amber Elmore
Charleston, WV

This is a delicious take on the classic tuna melt. I have enjoyed this lunch for years with a hot bowl of tomato soup. It's also tasty with sliced tomatoes and lettuce added after broiling.

5-oz. can tuna in water, drained and flaked
1 T. mayonnaise
1 t. mustard
cracked pepper to taste
4 slices whole-grain bread, toasted
2 slices American cheese

In a bowl, combine tuna, mayonnaise and mustard; season with pepper. For each sandwich, spread half of tuna mixture on one slice of toast; add a cheese slice and top with another slice of toast. Place on a broiler pan; broil just until cheese melts. Makes 2 servings.

Just a Bite FOR LUNCH

Althoff Italiano Salad

Miranda Althoff
Addieville, IL

My kids and I love salad, so we decided to make a version of our own. We had so much fun creating it together! A good side with it is homemade garlic bread made from hamburger buns broiled with garlic butter and a sprinkle of cheese.

3 heads romaine lettuce, chopped
3 roma tomatoes, sliced
1/4 c. red onion, diced
   and divided
1/2 c. jumbo black olives,
   cut into quarters
1-1/4 c. shredded Romano
   cheese
1 c. garlic salad dressing
1 c. garlic & cheese croutons
Garnish: extra chopped tomato,
   onion and black olives

In a large salad bowl, combine all ingredients except croutons and garnish. Toss with salad tongs to coat well. Top with croutons; garnish as desired. Makes 5 servings.

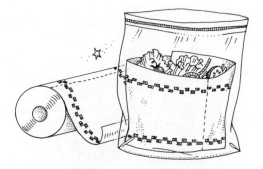

Keep salad greens fresh longer. Simply rinse and pat dry
as soon as they're brought home, wrap in a paper towel and
seal in a plastic zipping bag. The towel will absorb
any moisture and greens will stay crisp.

Mom's GO-TO *Recipes*

Spicy Tortellini Soup

Tiffany Jones
Batesville, AR

After birthday pictures and fun activities with my three-year-old twins, I needed a quick & easy meal. My goodness, was this delicious... my twins loved it! My daughter told me, "Mommy, you're the best cooker eber."

2 10-1/2 oz. cans beef broth
14-1/2 oz. can Italian-seasoned
   diced tomatoes
15-1/2 oz. can kidney beans,
   drained
14-1/2 oz. can sliced carrots,
   drained

7-oz. can green chiles, drained
1-1/4 oz. pkg. taco seasoning
   mix
1-oz. pkg. ranch seasoning mix
19-oz. pkg. frozen cheese
   tortellini, uncooked
8-oz. pkg. cream cheese, cubed

Combine broth, tomatoes with juice and remaining ingredients except tortellini and cream cheese in a soup pot. Bring to a boil over medium-high heat; stir in tortellini and cream cheese. Reduce heat to medium. Simmer until tortellini is cooked and cream cheese is melted, about 10 minutes. Makes 6 servings.

Surprisingly, canned tomatoes have even more health benefits than fresh tomatoes. With a few cans of already-seasoned tomatoes in the pantry, you can whip up a healthy and flavorful meal anytime.

Just a Bite FOR LUNCH

Tomato-Basil Soup

Carrolleen Hunt
Waynesboro, PA

I love hot soup for cold days and I love to sip this from a mug. In the wintertime, I make a pot of this soup every week.

2 T. onion, chopped
1 to 2 cloves garlic
2 T. butter
28-oz. can crushed tomatoes
10-3/4 oz. can tomato soup
2-1/2 c. chicken broth

1 T. sugar
3/4 c. half-and-half
2 T. fresh basil, chopped
2 T. fresh parsley, chopped
2 T. fresh chives, chopped
salt and pepper to taste

In a large saucepan over medium heat, sauté onion and garlic in butter. Transfer mixture to a blender; add tomatoes with juice and process until smooth. Return to saucepan; stir in soup, broth and sugar. Bring almost to a boil; reduce heat to medium-low. Stir in remaining ingredients. Simmer over low heat for for about 30 minutes, until flavors are blended. Makes 6 to 8 servings.

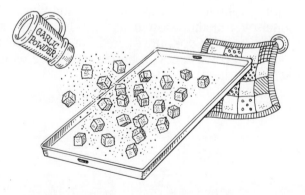

Make the most of leftover country-style bread...turn it into crispy croutons for soups and salads. Toss bread cubes with olive oil and chopped herbs. Toast on a baking sheet at 400 degrees for 5 to 10 minutes, until golden.

Grandma's Best Chili

Patricia Nau
River Grove, IL

My grandmother was a fantastic cook and baker. She made everything from scratch...a little bit of this & a handful of that. It took forever to get measurements for this! This recipe tastes just like Grandma's. It's the best chili, and one of my family's favorites.

3 lbs. ground beef chuck
2 12-oz. pkgs. frozen chopped
  onions
1 green pepper, chopped
2 t. garlic, chopped
2 T. chili powder
1 t. dried cumin
1 t. dried oregano
2 t. kosher salt
pepper to taste

14-1/2 oz. can diced tomatoes
2 6-oz. cans tomato paste
3 c. tomato juice
3 c. warm water
2 15-1/2 oz. cans dark red
  kidney beans, drained
Garnish: chopped onion,
  shredded Cheddar cheese, hot
  pepper sauce, saltine crackers

Brown beef in a large Dutch oven over medium heat; drain. Add onions, green pepper and garlic. Continue to sauté until onions are transparent. Add seasonings; adjust for taste. Cook and stir for 5 minutes. Stir in tomatoes with juice, tomato paste, tomato juice and warm water. Cover and simmer over medium-low heat for 1-1/2 hours, stirring occasionally. Stir in beans. Cook, uncovered, for 45 minutes. Add more tomato juice to desired consistency, if necessary. Serve with desired toppings. Makes 6 servings.

You can't have too much chili! Freeze leftovers in small containers, to be microwaved and spooned over hot dogs or baked potatoes for a quick & hearty lunch.

Just a Bite FOR LUNCH

Easy Beef Taco Soup

Brian Johnson
Springfield, OH

Very simple and easy to make.

1 lb. ground beef
2 10-oz. cans diced tomatoes
   with green chiles
15-1/2 oz. can black beans
15-1/2 oz. can Great Northern
   beans
15-1/2 oz. can red kidney beans
14-3/4 oz. can corn

1-1/4 oz. pkg. taco
   seasoning mix
1-oz. pkg. ranch salad
   dressing mix
Garnish: shredded taco-blend
   cheese, sour cream, tortilla
   chips

Brown beef in a stockpot over medium heat; drain. Add tomatoes with juice, beans and corn; do not drain any cans. Stir in seasoning mixes until blended. Simmer over medium-low heat for about one hour, stirring occasionally. Garnish with cheese, sour cream and tortilla chips. Makes 6 servings.

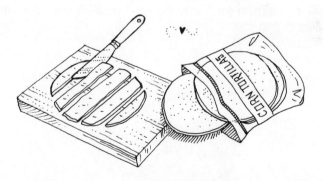

While the soup simmers, make some crunchy tortilla strip toppers. Brush or spray flour tortillas with olive oil on both sides. Cut the tortillas into narrow strips with a pizza cutter. Bake on a baking sheet at 375 degrees for 5 to 7 minutes, turning once or twice, until crisp and golden.

Mom's GO-TO Recipes

Spinach & White Bean Soup

Ann Tober
Biscoe, AR

This soup is so easy and so good...I always keep the ingredients for it on hand. I like to serve it with a pan of cornbread or garlic bread. A great warm-you-up meal!

1 T. olive oil
3 cloves garlic, minced
1 onion, diced
1/2 t. dried thyme
1/2 t. dried basil
4 c. chicken broth
1 c. water
2 bay leaves

1 c. orzo pasta, uncooked
2 15-1/2 oz. cans Great Northern
   beans, drained and rinsed
2 c. fresh baby spinach
juice of 1 lemon
2 T. fresh parsley, chopped
salt and pepper to taste

Heat olive oil in a Dutch oven over medium heat. Add garlic and onion; cook for 2 minutes, stirring often, until onion is translucent. Add thyme and basil; cook and stir for about one minute. Whisk in broth and water; add bay leaves and bring to a boil. Stir in orzo. Reduce heat to medium-low and simmer until orzo is tender, 10 to 12 minutes. Discard bay leaves. Add beans; stir in spinach and cook until wilted, about 2 minutes. Stir in lemon juice and parsley; season with salt and pepper. Makes 6 servings.

Post a notepad on the fridge to make a note whenever a pantry staple is used up. You'll never run out of that one item you need!

Just a Bite FOR LUNCH

Lentil & Sweet Potato Soup

Lisa Sett
Thousand Oaks, CA

My family loves this meatless soup. It's delicious
with warm cornbread.

7 c. vegetable broth or water
2 c. dried brown lentils, rinsed
   and sorted
3/4 c. onion, chopped
1/2 t. curry powder
1 bay leaf
salt and pepper to taste

2 sweet potatoes, peeled and
   cut into 1/2-inch cubes
14-1/2 oz. can diced tomatoes
2 carrots, peeled and chopped
2 stalks celery, chopped
2 zucchini, diced

Combine vegetable broth or water, lentils and onion in a large soup pot.
Bring to a boil over high heat; reduce heat to medium-low. Simmer for
10 minutes; stir in seasonings. Add sweet potatoes and cook until
tender, about 15 minutes. Add tomatoes with juice and remaining
vegetables. Simmer until tender, about 10 minutes. Remove bay leaf
and serve. Makes 6 servings.

Dried beans are healthful, inexpensive and come in lots of varieties...
perfect for delicious family meals. Before cooking, place beans in
a colander, rinse well and pick through, discarding any broken
beans and bits of debris.

Mom's GO-TO *Recipes*

Fruit & Nut Chicken Salad

Phyl Broich Wessling
Garner, IA

I make a double batch of this salad every year for our church's salad luncheon. There are never any leftovers!

4 c. cooked or grilled chicken, diced
11-oz. can mandarin oranges, drained
1-1/2 c. seedless green grapes, halved
1 c. celery, sliced
2-oz. pkg. slivered almonds, lightly toasted

1 c. mayonnaise
1/4 c. sour cream
1/8 t. garlic powder
1/2 t. salt
1/8 t. pepper
Garnish: lettuce leaves

Combine chicken, oranges, grapes, celery and almonds in a large bowl. In another bowl, combine mayonnaise, sour cream and seasonings. Pour mayonnaise mixture over chicken mixture; stir carefully. Cover and chill until serving time. Serve scoops of salad on lettuce leaves. Makes 8 to 10 servings.

Lillie's Fruit Salad

Margaret McNeil
Germantown, TN

My grandmother made this simple fruit salad for her children, my mother made it for her children and I make it for my children. It's kid-friendly, since most kids love all three fruits in the salad.

8-oz. can crushed pineapple in juice
2 ripe bananas, sliced

1 to 2 Red Delicious apples, cored and diced
1/2 c. orange juice

In a large bowl, combine all fruit. Add enough orange juice to cover fruit; mix gently. Cover and keep refrigerated. Serves 4 to 6.

A crockery bowl filled to the brim with ripe apples and pears makes a simple centerpiece...it's a great way to encourage healthy snacking too!

Just a Bite FOR LUNCH

Jane Doe Salad

Judy Taylor
Butler, MO

I have been making this salad for many years. It's something like a meatless taco salad. It never used to have a name, so my family began calling it Jane Doe Salad.

15-oz. can ranch-style beans, drained
8-oz. bottle Catalina salad dressing
1 head lettuce, chopped

2 tomatoes, chopped
1 bunch green onions, chopped
10-oz. pkg. sharp Cheddar cheese, cubed
6-oz. pkg. corn chips

Combine beans and salad dressing in a bowl. Cover and refrigerate at least 4 hours. Shortly before serving time, combine lettuce, tomatoes, onions and cheese in a salad bowl. Spoon bean mixture over top; toss thoroughly. Finely crush corn chips in bag; mix into salad just before serving. Makes 8 servings.

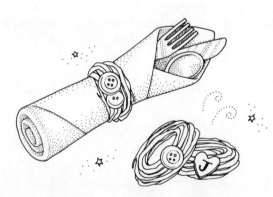

Cloth napkins make mealtime just a little more special...and they're a must when serving soup! Stitch or hot-glue fun charms to napkin rings so everyone can identify their own napkin easily.

Mom's GO-TO *Recipes*

Cheesy Burger Soup

Crystal Shook
Catawba, NC

*One of my son's favorite comfort foods. Great served
in homemade bread bowls!*

1 lb. ground beef
4 T. butter, divided
3/4 c. onion, chopped
3/4 c. carrots, peeled and
   shredded
3/4 c. celery, diced
1 t. dried basil
1. t. dried parsley
3 c. chicken broth

4 c. potatoes, peeled and diced
1/4 c. all-purpose flour
8-oz. pkg. pasteurized process
   cheese, cubed
1-1/2 c. milk
3/4 t. salt
1/4 t. pepper
1/4 c. sour cream

Brown beef in a skillet over medium heat; drain and set aside.
Meanwhile, in a soup pot, melt one tablespoon butter over medium
heat. Sauté onion, carrots, celery, basil and parsley until vegetables
are tender. Add broth, potatoes and beef; bring to a boil. Reduce heat
to medium-low and simmer for 10 to 12 minutes, until potatoes are
tender. Melt remaining butter in a small skillet over medium heat;
sprinkle with flour. Cook, stirring often, for 3 to 5 minutes, until bubbly.
Add to soup; bring to a boil. Cook and stir for 2 minutes. Reduce heat
to low. Add cheese, milk and seasonings; cook until cheese melts. Blend
in sour cream. Makes 8 servings.

Have crayon masterpieces taken over the refrigerator? Select a few
special drawings to be matted and framed...the kids will be so proud!

Just a Bite FOR LUNCH

Spinach-Beef Soup with Bowties
Gladys Kielar
Whitehouse, OH

*There's nothing more comforting than a bowl of this
beefy soup during the cold weather days.*

1 lb. ground beef
3 cloves garlic, minced
2 32-oz. containers reduced-
   sodium beef broth
2 14-1/2 oz. cans diced tomatoes
   with green peppers, celery
   and onion

1 t. dried basil
1/2 t. dried oregano
1/2 t. pepper
3 c. mini bowtie pasta, uncooked
4 c. fresh spinach, coarsely
   chopped
Garnish: grated Parmesan cheese

In a large stockpot over medium heat, cook beef and garlic for
6 to 8 minutes, until beef is no longer pink, breaking up into crumbles.
Drain. Stir in broth, tomatoes with juice and seasonings; bring to a boil.
Stir in pasta; return to a boil. Cook, uncovered, for 7 to 9 minutes, until
pasta is tender. Stir in spinach; cook until wilted. Sprinkle servings with
cheese. Makes 8 servings.

For speedy meal prep, set a bowl on the kitchen counter to collect
scraps and trimmings while you cook. Then just make one trip
to the trash can when you're done.

Mom's GO-TO *Recipes*

Super Philly Beef Sandwich

Sue Klapper
Muskego, WI

I love to make this sandwich for our weekly sandwich night. It's yummy and quick to prepare.

2 T. margarine
1/2 c. onion, coarsely chopped
1-1/2 c. sliced mushrooms
1/3 c. green pepper, chopped

4 kaiser rolls, split
1/4 lb. thinly sliced deli roast
  beef
4 slices Provolone cheese

Melt margarine in a skillet over medium-high heat; add onion, mushrooms and green pepper. Cook for 5 minutes, stirring occasionally, until tender. Place bottom halves of rolls on an ungreased baking sheet. Toast under broiler, if desired. Top with vegetable mixture, beef and cheese. Broil for 2 to 3 minutes, just until cheese melts. Add tops of rolls, toasted if desired. Makes 4 servings.

Grilled Reuben Sandwich

Patty Flak
Erie, PA

So easy and so delicious when you want something a little heartier than grilled cheese.

2 slices marble rye bread
2 T. Thousand Island salad
  dressing
1 slice Swiss cheese

2 slices deli corned beef
1/4 c. sauerkraut, rinsed
  and drained
softened butter to taste

Spread one slice of bread with salad dressing; layer with cheese and corned beef. Top with sauerkraut and remaining bread slice. Spread outside of sandwich with butter. Spray a skillet with non-stick vegetable spray; heat over medium-high heat. Add sandwich to skillet. Cook, turning once, until toasted, golden and cheese is melted. Makes one serving.

Just for kids...serve cut-up veggies with small cups of peanut butter, ranch dressing or hummus for dipping.

Just a Bite FOR LUNCH

Cheeseburger Joes

Jenny Devening
Freetown, IN

This is a super-easy recipe that cooks up in no time. Serve with French fries or potato chips...yum!

1 lb. lean ground beef
1/2 c. barbecue sauce
1/4 c. catsup

4 hamburger buns, split
4 slices American cheese

Brown beef in a skillet over medium heat; drain. Stir in barbecue sauce and catsup; heat through. To serve, spoon onto hamburger buns; top with a cheese slice and serve. Makes 4 servings.

Cheese & Wiener Crescents

Leona Krivda
Belle Vernon, PA

These are so simple, but my son Kevin loves them! Growing up, he was a happy kid with one of these and baked beans on the side.

8-oz. tube refrigerated crescent
   rolls, separated
8 hot dogs, split down the middle
8 slices American cheese, each
   cut in half

Garnish: mustard, catsup or
   other dipping sauce

Lay out each crescent roll; place a hot dog across the wide end. Insert a cheese slice in slit in hot dog. Roll up crescent rolls, starting at the wide end. Arrange point-side down on a lightly greased baking sheet. Bake at 375 degrees for 12 to 15 minutes. Serve warm with favorite dipping sauce. Serves 8.

To show a child what once delighted you,
to find the child's delight added to
your own, this is happiness.

– J.B. Priestley

Mom's GO-TO *Recipes*

Connie's Black Bean & Corn Chili
Betsy Smith
McKinney, TX

Miss Connie, who lives in Pensacola, Florida and is a very good family friend, shared this recipe with me for a quick and delicious weeknight dinner. It is one of my favorite go-to chili recipes...and, I might add, a "Connie Original"! I serve it with hot cornbread. This is a divine recipe and is so easy!

1 to 1-1/2 lbs. ground beef
    sirloin or chuck
1 c. celery, diced
1 c. yellow onion, diced
2 T. olive oil
14-1/2 oz. can diced tomatoes
    with green chiles

15-1/2 oz. can black beans
10-oz. pkg. frozen corn
10-3/4 oz. can tomato soup
10-3/4 oz. can tomato
    bisque soup
1-oz. pkg. chili seasoning mix
1 c. water

Brown beef in a skillet over medium heat; drain. Transfer to a large stockpot and set aside. In the same skillet, sauté celery and onion in olive oil; add to beef. Stir in tomatoes with juice and remaining ingredients. Simmer over medium heat until heated through, stirring occasionally. Add a little more water, if needed. Makes 10 to 12 servings.

Stretch a pot of chili to feed even more people...serve it Cincinnati-style! For 2-way chili, ladle chili over a bowl of spaghetti. For 3-way, top chili and spaghetti with shredded cheese. For 4-way, spoon diced onions on top of the cheese...add chili beans to the stack for 5-way. Scrumptious!

Just a Bite FOR LUNCH

Chicken Taco Soup in a Flash

Velma Salzman
Leakey, TX

This soup was a go-to meal at our house on weekday evenings after running the kids to practice. Especially yummy on wet, dreary days, but good anytime. It's a snap to put together!

12-oz. can chicken, drained
    and flaked
14-1/2 oz. can diced tomatoes
    with mild green chiles,
    drained
15-1/4 oz. can corn, drained
15-oz. can ranch-style beans
14-1/2 oz. can chicken broth
8-oz. can tomato sauce

1 avocado, peeled, pitted
    and diced
1/8 t. onion powder
1/8 t. garlic powder
8-oz. container sour cream
8-oz. pkg shredded Cheddar
    cheese, divided
6-oz. pkg. tortilla chips

Combine chicken, tomatoes, corn and beans in a large soup pot over medium heat. Add broth, tomato sauce and avocado; bring to a boil. Remove from heat; stir in seasonings, sour cream and one cup cheese. To serve, crumble tortilla chips into bowls. Ladle soup over chips; top with remaining cheese. Makes 6 to 8 servings.

¡olé!

Cheesy quesadillas are quick and filling paired with a bowl of soup. Sprinkle a flour tortilla with shredded cheese, top with another tortilla and toast lightly in a skillet until the cheese melts. Cut into wedges and serve with salsa.

Pepperoni Pizza Braid

Carla Slajchert
Bellevue, NE

This is a recipe I came up with when we wanted something fun for lunch, but didn't want to fuss with making pizza. My kids gobbled it up and declared it a winner! I usually top with whatever we have on hand. Pepperoni and mushrooms are a favorite combination.

1 lb. pizza crust dough, thawed
   if frozen
15-oz. jar pizza sauce, divided
1-1/4 c. shredded mozzarella
   cheese, divided

18 pepperoni slices
1 t. Italian seasoning
1 T. olive oil
2 T. grated Parmesan cheese

On a floured surface, roll pizza dough into a 13-inch by 7-inch rectangle. Transfer dough to a lightly greased baking sheet. Spread 1/2 cup pizza sauce lengthwise down the center of dough. Sprinkle half of mozzarella cheese over sauce. Layer pepperoni over mozzarella. Sprinkle seasoning over pepperoni; sprinkle with remaining mozzarella. On the long edges of dough, cut slits horizontally all the way to sauce mixture. Lift slits and place over toppings, alternating left and right in a criss-cross style. Drizzle with olive oil; sprinkle with Parmesan cheese. Bake at 400 degrees for 15 to 18 minutes, until golden and cheese is melted. Warm remaining pizza sauce in a small saucepan over low heat; serve with braid for dipping. Serves 4 to 6.

Keep a cherished cookbook clean and free of spatters. Slip it into a gallon-size plastic zipping bag before cooking up a favorite recipe.

Just a Bite FOR LUNCH

Mary's Broccoli-Cauliflower Salad

Mary Warren
Sanford, MI

A friend at work shared this recipe with me years ago. I made a couple of changes to make it my own. My family loves it and I've shared it many times with relatives and friends. You can use all broccoli or all cauliflower, if you like. It's a recipe that can be served at any occasion and is always well received.

1/2 lb. bacon, crisply cooked
    and crumbled
1/2 bunch broccoli, cut into
    flowerets
1/2 head cauliflower, cut into
    flowerets

1-1/2 to 2 c. shredded
    Cheddar cheese
3 to 4 T. green onions or
    sweet onion, diced

Combine all ingredients in a large bowl; toss to mix. Drizzle with Dressing; toss to coat well. Cover and refrigerate until serving time. Makes 6 to 8 servings.

Dressing:

1 c. mayonnaise-type salad
    dressing

2 T. white vinegar
1/3 c. sugar or sugar substitute

Combine all ingredients; whisk until blended.

Keep a pair of kitchen scissors handy! They make quick work of chopping green onions, snipping fresh herbs and opening packages.

Mom's GO-TO Recipes

My Sister's Chicken Soup

Sheila Murray
Tehachapi, CA

Comfort soup for a nice cool day. I prefer to cook the rice or noodles separately, so they don't soak up all the broth.

8 c. water
6 cubes chicken bouillon
4 boneless, skinless chicken
   breasts
4 stalks celery, chopped
4 carrots, peeled and chopped
1 onion, chopped

4 cloves garlic, pressed
1 bay leaf
3/4 t. pepper
juice of 1/2 lemon
1/2 c. long-cooking rice or
   1 c. narrow egg noodles,
   cooked

In a large soup pot over medium-high heat, combine water and bouillon cubes. Bring to a boil; stir well. Add remaining ingredients except rice or noodles. Reduce heat to medium-low. Cover and simmer for 1-1/2 to 2 hours, stirring occasionally and adding more water, if needed. Remove chicken to a bowl; cool, shred and return to soup. Discard bay leaf; stir in cooked rice or noodles. Makes 4 to 6 servings.

Are the kids bored, waiting for dinner? A package of refrigerated bread sticks presents all kinds of alphabet fun...just shape the dough into letters before baking! Sprinkle with Parmesan cheese or cinnamon-sugar for a special treat.

Just a Bite FOR LUNCH

Cheesy Vegetable Chowder

Charlotte Smith
Tyrone, PA

This recipe is so delicious and a family favorite. Even if your children don't like veggies, they'll love this soup!

2 T. butter
1/2 c. onion, chopped
1 c. carrots, peeled and finely
   chopped
1 stalk celery, finely chopped
1 T. garlic, minced
4 c. chicken broth

2 potatoes, peeled and diced
1 T. all-purpose flour
1/2 c. cold water
2/3 c. milk
2 c. broccoli, chopped
8-oz. pkg. shredded Cheddar
   cheese

Melt butter in a large soup pot over medium heat. Add onion, carrots and celery; sauté until tender. Add garlic and cook for to 2 minutes. Add broth and potatoes; bring to a boil. Reduce heat to medium-low; simmer until potatoes are tender. Mix flour with water in a bowl; stir into soup. Simmer until soup is slightly thickened. Stir in milk and broccoli; cook until broccoli is just tender and soup is heated through. Add cheese; stir until melted. Makes 6 servings.

Make your own flavorful vegetable broth. Save up veggie scraps and trimmings in the freezer. When you have enough, cover with water in a soup pot and simmer gently for 30 minutes. Strain and use for your next pot of soup.

Mom's GO-TO *Recipes*

Sunshine Daycare Vegetable Beef Soup

Beth Bundy
Long Prairie, MN

My mom was the best cook ever! Many years ago, she worked at a daycare center. This soup was her brilliant way to get the children to eat their veggies. So simple to make and beyond delicious!

1 lb. ground beef
1/2 c. onion, chopped
5 c. water
4 cubes beef bouillon
16-oz. pkg. frozen mixed
    vegetables

3 c. potatoes, peeled and diced
8-oz. can tomato sauce
1 t. garlic powder
salt and pepper to taste

Brown beef with onion in a skillet over medium heat; drain. Meanwhile, in a soup pot over medium-high heat, bring water and bouillon cubes to a boil. Stir in beef and remaining ingredients. Cover and simmer over low heat for 2 hours, stirring occasionally. Serves 6.

Seasoned Oyster Crackers

Roberta Simpkins
Mentor on the Lake, OH

This recipe was given to my mom years ago and we continue to make it for family gatherings. Great for soups and snacking!

2 9-oz. pkgs. oyster crackers
1 c. popcorn popping oil
1 T. dill weed

1/2 t. garlic powder
1-oz. pkg. ranch salad dressing
    mix

Spread crackers on a large baking sheet; set aside. In a bowl, whisk together remaining ingredients; drizzle over crackers. Let stand for several hours; transfer to an airtight container. Serves 8 to 10.

A comfortable house is
a great source of happiness.
– Sydney Smith

Just a Bite FOR LUNCH

Confetti Coleslaw

Dale Evans
Frankfort, MI

For an extra-special garnish, cut slits lengthwise in green onions and arrange on top of the coleslaw...mandarin orange sections placed at the tip of each green onion will resemble a flower.

3 c. coleslaw mix
3/4 c. frozen corn, cooked
   and drained
1/4 c. red pepper, diced
1/4 c. green pepper, diced
4 T. green onions, chopped and
   divided

11-oz. can mandarin oranges,
   drained and divided
1/2 c. mayonnaise
2 T. sugar
1 T. raspberry vinegar
1 T. lime or lemon juice

Combine coleslaw mix, corn, red pepper, green pepper, 3 tablespoons green onions and oranges, reserving 6 orange sections for garnish. Mix together mayonnaise, sugar, vinegar and juice; blend well. Pour over salad and toss to coat well. Transfer to serving dish. Garnish with reserved orange. Serves 8.

Short on time? Make tonight sandwich night! Pick up some sandwich bread or buns and favorite deli meats and cheeses...let everyone fix sandwiches their way. A make-ahead salad like Family Favorite Coleslaw is easy to pull out and serve at mealtime.

Mom's GO-TO Recipes

Momma's Cheesy Potato Soup

Lori Peterson
Effingham, KS

While I was visiting my mom one chilly evening, she started tossing things together in a soup pot. She came up with the best-tasting potato soup!

1 c. onion, chopped
1/4 c. butter
6 c. potatoes, peeled and diced
1 c. carrots, peeled and diced
10-3/4 oz. can cream of
    chicken soup

8-oz. container sour cream
8-oz. pkg. Cheddar cheese,
    cubed
salt and pepper to taste

In a soup pot over medium heat, sauté onion in butter until tender. Add potatoes, carrots and just enough water to cover vegetables; bring to a boil. Reduce heat to medium-low and simmer until vegetables are tender. Stir in remaining ingredients. Cook over medium to low heat, stirring occasionally, until cheese is melted. Serves 6.

Need a quick after-school snack for the kids? Nothing beats popcorn! To add new flavor, sprinkle popcorn with taco seasoning or grated Parmesan cheese before filling snack-size plastic bags.

Just a Bite FOR LUNCH

Simple Cabbage-Sausage Soup

Angela Bissette
Middlesex, NC

This is a delicious, hearty soup perfect for cool weather.
It's excellent served with homemade bread or rolls.

1 lb. Kielbasa or smoked
   sausage, sliced
2 T. oil
14-1/2 oz. can stewed tomatoes
14-1/2 oz. can chicken broth

4 potatoes, peeled and diced
1 head cabbage, coarsely
   chopped
3/4 c. onion, diced
salt and pepper to taste

In a large soup pot over medium heat, cook sausage in oil until lightly browned. Stir in tomatoes with juice and remaining ingredients; bring to a boil. Reduce heat to medium-low. Cover and simmer for 30 minutes, or until vegetables are tender. Serves 8.

Creamy Potato & Kale Soup

Laura Flood
Markleville, IN

My family loves this soup!

6 to 8 potatoes, peeled and cubed
16-oz. pkg. ground pork
   sausage, browned and
   drained
3 c. fresh kale, chopped
2 c. chicken broth

1 c. milk
1/2 c. half-and-half
1 t. salt
1 t. pepper
1 t. red pepper flakes

In a large soup pot over medium heat, cover potatoes with water. Cook until tender, about 15 minutes; do not drain. Stir in remaining ingredients. Simmer over medium-low heat for 20 minutes; do not boil. Makes 6 to 8 servings.

If the soup boils over, cover cooked-on food spots on the stove with equal parts of water and baking soda. Spills will soak right off!

Mom's **GO-TO** *Recipes*

Corn & Ham Chowder

Marian Forck
Chamois, MO

I love to cook and make up my own recipes...and I love to eat soup on a chilly day! Serve with homemade bread and butter for a great filling meal.

1 lb. cooked ham, cubed
1 c. onion, chopped
1/4 c. celery, chopped
1 T. oil
4 c. potatoes, peeled and cut into
    1/2-inch cubes
2 c. water

1/2 t. dried marjoram
1 t. salt
1/8 t. pepper
12-oz. can evaporated milk
15-1/4 oz. can corn, drained
14-3/4 oz. can creamed corn

In a Dutch oven over medium heat, cook ham, onion and celery in oil until vegetables are tender. Drain mixture on paper towels; return to Dutch oven. Stir in potatoes, water and seasonings; bring to a boil. Reduce heat to medium-low. Simmer, uncovered, about 15 to 20 minutes, until potatoes are tender. Stir in milk and corn; heat through. Makes 6 servings.

A fun way to serve cornbread...waffle wedges or strips! Mix up the batter, thin it slightly with a little extra milk, then bake in a waffle iron until crisp. Terrific for dunking in soup or chili!

Skillet &
Stovetop
SUPPERS

Mom's GO-TO *Recipes*

Stir-Fry Beef & Veggies

Leona Krivda
Belle Vernon, PA

*This recipe was given to me many years ago. I made it often,
as my children always enjoyed it.*

1-1/2 lbs. beef round or sirloin
  steak, cut into thin strips
1/4 c. oil
1/2 c. onion, thinly sliced
1 green pepper, cut into
  thin strips
1 c. celery, thinly sliced
1 c. sliced mushrooms

3/4 c. carrots, peeled and
  thinly sliced
1 T. cornstarch
1/4 c. low-sodium soy sauce
8-oz. can tomato sauce
1 t. sugar
cooked rice

In a large skillet over high heat, brown beef in oil. Add onion, green
pepper, celery, mushrooms and carrots; cook until tender-crisp. In a
bowl, blend cornstarch with soy sauce; stir in tomato sauce and sugar.
Add soy sauce mixture to beef mixture. Cook and stir for 3 to 4 minutes,
until sauce thickens slightly. To serve, spoon over cooked rice. Makes
4 to 6 servings.

One-pot meals are a busy mom's best friend! Stir-Fry Beef & Veggies
is a great example. Whether made on the stovetop, in the oven or
in a slow cooker, they're your best choice for making mealtime
easier...fewer pots & pans to wash too! You'll find lots of
one-pot choices throughout this book.

Skillet & Stovetop SUPPERS

Chicken with Sun-Dried Tomatoes

Shirley Howie
Foxboro, MA

This makes a great quick & easy weeknight dinner. Sometimes I'll substitute thyme or oregano for the basil...any of these herbs will complement the flavor of the sun-dried tomatoes.

3 T. olive oil, divided
4 boneless, skinless chicken
  breasts
1/2 c. onion, chopped
10-3/4 oz. can cream of
  mushroom soup
3/4 c. water

1/4 c. sun-dried tomatoes in oil,
  drained and thinly sliced
1 T. red wine vinegar
1 t. dried basil
cooked wide egg noodles
Garnish: shredded Parmesan
  cheese

Heat 2 tablespoons olive oil in a skillet over medium-high heat. Add chicken and cook for 10 minutes, or until well browned on both sides. Remove chicken from skillet; set aside. Heat remaining oil in skillet. Add onion; cook and stir for 2 minutes. Add soup, water, tomatoes, vinegar and basil to skillet; stir to combine. Return chicken to skillet; bring to a boil. Reduce heat to low; cover and cook for about 10 minutes, until chicken is cooked through. Serve chicken and sauce over cooked noodles, sprinkled with Parmesan cheese. Serves 4.

When browning meat, don't overcrowd the skillet. Add cubes or strips in 2 to 3 batches, turning pieces occasionally, and removing to a plate while browning the rest.

Mom's GO-TO *Recipes*

Garden Stir-Fry with Sausage

Sharon Adams
Bainbridge, OH

*My friend brought this yummy dish to a get-together late one
summer to use up some of her garden veggies. I took a plate
home to my hubby and now he requests it all year long!*

2 T. oil
1 lb. smoked pork sausage,
   cut into chunks
1/2 to 1 head cabbage,
   thinly sliced
1 c. broccoli, chopped

3/4 c. carrots, peeled and
   thinly sliced
1 zucchini, cubed
1 yellow squash, cubed
14-1/2 oz. can Italian-style diced
   tomatoes

Heat oil in a large skillet over medium-high heat; add all ingredients
except tomatoes. Cook, stirring constantly, to desired tenderness. Add
tomatoes with juice; cook and stir until heated through. Makes 4 to
6 servings.

One-Pot Pork Chop Dinner

Sandy Coffey
Cincinnati, OH

*This is an old recipe that's great for busy school nights.
Serve with a crisp salad and hot buttered rolls.*

1 T. butter
4 pork chops
4 carrots, peeled and cut
   into chunks
3 potatoes, peeled and quartered

1 onion, sliced
10-3/4 oz. can cream of
   mushroom soup
1/2 c. water
1/2 t. salt

Melt butter in a skillet over medium heat; brown pork chops for 3 to 5
minutes on each side. Add potatoes, carrots and onion to skillet. In a
bowl, combine soup, water and salt; add to skillet. Cover and simmer for
15 to 20 minutes, until vegetables are tender. Makes 4 servings.

Protect non-stick skillets from
scratches when stacked in a
cupboard...slip a paper plate or
coffee filter in between them.

Skillet & Stovetop SUPPERS

Easy Chicken & Vegetables

Wendy Bjorklund
Olympia, WA

Here's a recipe I love to make! As a working person, I love kitchen shortcuts...rotisserie chicken is such a nice convenience and so tasty. With cooked rice or mashed potatoes, it's a quick tasty dinner.

2 T. butter
3/4 c. onion, finely chopped
3/4 c. celery, sliced
3/4 c. carrots, peeled and finely
   chopped
2 14-1/2 oz. cans chicken broth

1/2 c. all-purpose flour
1/2 c. cold water
2 c. deli rotisserie chicken,
   chopped
cooked rice or mashed potatoes

In a large non-stick skillet, melt butter over medium heat. Add onion; cook until beginning to soften, about 3 minutes. Add celery and carrots; cook for 3 more minutes. Add broth; simmer until vegetables are tender, about 10 more minutes. In a lidded jar, combine flour with cold water; shake to combine. Pour through a strainer into simmering vegetables; cook and stir to desired thickness. Add chicken; cook until just heated through. Serve mixture over cooked rice or mashed potatoes. Serves 4.

Shop for seasonal produce at farmers' markets...corn and tomatoes in summer, acorn squash and pears in fall, cabbage and apples in winter and strawberries and asparagus in spring. You'll be serving your family the freshest fruits & veggies year 'round.

Mom's GO-TO *Recipes*

Skillet Lasagna

Christine Lamb
Euless, TX

*No oven needed! Just a few ingredients and your stovetop
is all you need to cook this tasty lasagna.*

1 lb. ground beef
1 T. Worcestershire sauce
salt and pepper to taste
1/2 c. onion, chopped
1/2 green pepper, chopped
2 8-oz. cans tomato sauce

14-1/2 oz. can diced tomatoes
1 T. Italian seasoning
1-1/2 c. water
4 lasagna noodles, uncooked and
    broken into pieces
1/4 c. grated Parmesan cheese

Cook beef in a skillet over medium-high heat; drain. Stir in
Worcestershire sauce, salt and pepper. Crumble beef; cook until no
longer pink. Add onion and green pepper; cook and stir for 2 minutes.
Stir in tomato sauce, tomatoes with juice, seasoning and water; bring
to a boil. Stir in noodles; reduce heat to medium and simmer for
10 minutes, or until noodles are tender. Remove from heat; stir in
cheese before serving. Serves 4.

Mix up your own Italian seasoning to store in a big shaker jar...
you probably already have the ingredients in your spice rack! A good
basic blend is 2 tablespoons each of dried oregano, basil, thyme,
marjoram and rosemary. Add or subtract to suit your family's taste.

Skillet & Stovetop
SUPPERS

Zucchini & Yellow Squash Medley

Melanie Johnston
Wilton, NH

This is a fresh and healthy veggie side dish, especially nice during a cool summer's evening barbecue.

1-1/2 t. olive oil
1/2 onion, chopped
3 zucchini, sliced
3 yellow squash, sliced

14-1/2 oz. can diced seasoned
  tomatoes with basil,
  garlic & oregano

Heat olive oil in a large skillet over medium-high heat; cook onion until golden. Add zucchini, squash and tomatoes with juice. Cover and cook over medium-low heat until tender. Serves 4 to 6.

Tangy Green Beans

Mary Keene
Keaau, HI

The original recipe was given to me in my seventh-grade cooking class. I've simplified it, as it needs very little extra flavor.

1-1/2 to 2 c. fresh green beans,
  trimmed, or 14-1/2 oz. can
  green beans, drained

1 T. butter, melted
1 to 3 t. Worcestershire sauce
1 to 3 t. mustard

If using fresh green beans, steam until tender. Combine remaining ingredients in a saucepan over medium heat. Add green beans; stir gently to coat. Simmer for 10 minutes. Serves 2 to 3.

Can't remember if you've already tried a recipe? Start adding a little smiley face in the page's margin for recipes you've tried... you'll remember if it was a hit!

Mom's GO-TO *Recipes*

Best Chicken Stir-Fry

Rita Goad
Edmond, OK

This is a real family favorite! This recipe goes together so smoothly when all the cutting and chopping is done first. Then it is quick & easy, taking only 20 minutes or so to cook.

16-oz. pkg. angel hair pasta,
  uncooked
4 c. broccoli flowerets
8-oz. bottle Asian sesame
  salad dressing
1/3 c. soy sauce
1/2 t. ground ginger
1/2 t. garlic powder
1/2 t. cayenne pepper

2 to 3 t. oil
2 lbs. boneless, skinless
  chicken, cubed
1 bunch green onions, chopped
1 bunch fresh cilantro, chopped
20-oz. can pineapple tidbits,
  drained
Garnish: dry-roasted salted
  peanuts

Break pasta into pieces, 2 to 3 inches long. Cook pasta according to package directions, adding broccoli for last 3 minutes of cooking time. Drain and set aside. Meanwhile, in a bowl, mix together salad dressing, soy sauce and seasonings; set aside. Heat oil in a large non-stick skillet over medium-high heat. Add chicken and cook for 6 to 8 minutes, until lightly golden and cooked through. Add dressing mixture to skillet. Cook for one minute, stirring occasionally. Add onions, cilantro and pineapple; cook until onions and cilantro are wilted. Add chicken mixture to pasta mixture; toss lightly. Serve topped with peanuts. Makes about 8 servings.

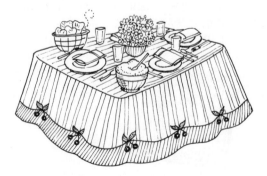

Take time to share family stories and traditions with your kids over the dinner table. A cherished family recipe can be a super conversation starter.

Skillet & Stovetop
SUPPERS

Stir-Fry Chicken &
Angel Hair Pasta

Jen Licon-Connor
Gooseberry Patch

Yum! This is one of our family's favorite meals. My kids are old enough now to help cut up veggies for it...pretty soon, they'll take over cooking it!

16-oz. pkg. angel hair pasta, uncooked
4 T. oil, divided
2 cloves garlic, minced
1 T. fresh ginger, peeled and grated
1 lb. boneless, skinless chicken breasts, sliced
3 carrots, peeled and sliced
1 bunch broccoli, cut into small flowerets
2 c. cauliflower, cut into small flowerets
5-oz. pkg. baby spinach
1/2 c. green onions, chopped
1/2 c. red wine vinegar
2 T. soy sauce

Cook pasta according to package directions; drain. Transfer to a large bowl and set aside. Meanwhile, in a large skillet over medium heat, heat 2 tablespoons oil. Add garlic and ginger; sauté for one minute. Add chicken; cook and stir for 5 minutes. Add carrots, broccoli and cauliflower; cook and stir for 4 to 5 minutes. Add spinach and onions; cook and stir until spinach wilts. Add chicken mixture to pasta; set aside. Add remaining oil, vinegar and soy sauce to skillet; simmer for one to 2 minutes. Drizzle oil mixture over chicken mixture; toss to mix well and serve. Makes 6 to 8 servings.

When chopping ingredients, be sure not to mix fresh veggies and raw meat on the same cutting board. Use 2 separate cutting boards, or wash the cutting board well in between ingredients.

Dad's Favorite Lemon Chicken Cutlets

Gladys Kielar
Whitehouse, OH

My husband Ed makes this recipe. It is his favorite choice when he's making dinner for us. Serve it over cooked rice or pasta...delicious.

6 boneless, skinless chicken
    breasts
1/2 c. all-purpose flour
1/2 t. salt
1/8 t. pepper

3 T. butter
1 c. boiling water
1 cube chicken bouillon
juice of 1/2 lemon
2 small lemons, thinly sliced

Place chicken breasts between 2 pieces of plastic wrap; pound until about 1/4-inch thick. Combine flour, salt and pepper in a shallow dish; coat chicken on both sides. Reserve remaining flour mixture. Melt butter in a large skillet over medium-high heat. Add chicken; brown lightly on both sides and remove to a plate. Reduce heat to medium-low. Stir remaining flour mixture into drippings; add water, bouillon cube and lemon juice. Return chicken to skillet; top with lemon slices. Cover and simmer for 5 minutes, or until chicken is fork-tender. Makes 6 servings.

Need a quick, tasty side? Stir sautéed diced mushrooms, onion or celery into prepared wild rice mix for a homemade touch.

Skillet & Stovetop
SUPPERS

Skillet Potato Pie

Shirl Parsons
Cape Carteret, NC

Looks like lots more effort than it is!

1-1/2 lbs. redskin potatoes,
  boiled
1/2 c. buttermilk

2 green onions, minced
salt and pepper to taste
oil for frying

Slice potatoes 1/4-inch thick. Place in a bowl; mash lightly just until broken up. Stir in buttermilk and green onions; season with salt and pepper. In a non-stick skillet over medium heat, heat just enough oil to coat skillet. Spoon potato mixture into skillet; pat evenly. Cook until potatoes are crisp and golden on the bottom. Slide out onto a plate and cut into wedges. Serves 4.

Sautéed Asparagus

Rosemary Lightbown
Wakefield, RI

Our garden produces more and more asparagus each year.
This is a welcome addition to any meal.

1/4 c. butter
2 T. olive oil
1 t. salt
1/4 t. pepper

3 cloves garlic, minced
1 lb. fresh asparagus, trimmed
1/2 lemon

Melt butter in a large skillet over medium heat; stir in oil, salt and pepper. Add garlic; cook for one minute. Add asparagus; cook for 10 to 12 minutes, until tender. Add a squeeze of lemon juice before serving. Makes 4 servings.

Freshly grated citrus zest adds so much flavor! Whenever you use a lemon or lime, just grate the peel first. Keep it frozen in an airtight container up to 2 months.

Mom's GO-TO *Recipes*

Gobblin' Good Turkey Burgers

Brandi Glenn
Los Osos, CA

This was my mom's recipe...I'll take these over
plain old hamburgers any day!

1 lb. ground turkey
1 onion, minced
1 c. shredded Cheddar cheese
1/4 c. Worcestershire sauce
1/2 t. dry mustard

salt and pepper to taste
6 to 8 hamburger buns, split
Garnish: lettuce leaves,
  sliced tomatoes

Combine all ingredients except buns; form into 4 to 6 patties. Grill to desired doneness; serve on hamburger buns. Garnish as desired. Makes 4 to 6 sandwiches.

Sandwich buns just taste better toasted...and they won't get soggy! Preheat a skillet over medium heat. Butter the cut sides of buns generously and place them butter-side down in the hot skillet. Cook for about 10 seconds, until toasty and golden. Serve warm.

Honey Baked Beans

Jill Ball
Highland, UT

We love barbecues...in the canyon, on the beach or in our own backyard. And no barbecue is complete without baked beans! This is our favorite recipe. It is easy to make and delicious to eat.

2 16-oz. cans baked beans
4 slices bacon, crisply cooked
   and crumbled
3/4 c. barbecue sauce

2 T. onion, chopped
2 T. honey
3/4 t. paprika
1/4 t. dry mustard

Combine all ingredients in a saucepan over medium-low heat. Cover and simmer for 30 to 45 minutes, stirring occasionally. Makes 10 to 12 servings.

Keep bacon drippings in a jar in the fridge. Add a spoonful or 2 when cooking hashbrown potatoes, green beans or pan gravy for wonderful down-home flavor.

Mom's GO-TO Recipes

Swiss Steak Supper

Lorissa Hiebert
Manitoba, Canada

*My family loves this recipe...it's an all-time favorite and
a great one-dish dinner! The ingredients combine to create
such a wonderful flavor together. It is a must-try.*

1/4 c. all-purpose flour
1 t. salt
1/4 t. pepper
1-1/2 lbs. beef round steak,
    cut into serving-size pieces
1 T. oil
28-oz. can diced tomatoes
3/4 c. onion, sliced

4-oz. can whole green chiles,
    drained
4 redskin potatoes, peeled
    and quartered
4 carrots, peeled and cut into
    2-inch chunks
2 T. cornstarch
2 T. cold water

In a large plastic zipping bag, combine flour, salt, and pepper. Add steak
and shake to coat; set aside. Heat oil in a skillet over medium heat; add
steak pieces and brown on both sides. Add tomatoes with juice and
onion to skillet; spoon chiles over steak. Bring to a boil. Reduce heat
to medium-low; cover and simmer for 30 minutes. Add potatoes and
carrots to skillet. Cover and simmer for 70 to 80 minutes, until steak
and vegetables are tender. Combine cornstarch and water in a small jar;
shake until smooth and stir into mixture in skillet. Bring to a boil,
stirring constantly, until thickened and bubbly. Serves 5.

To give a nutritious boost to recipes, add finely minced veggies
to your family's favorite dishes....they'll blend right in!

Homestyle Cheeseburger Macaroni Dish

Beckie Apple
Grannis, AR

My family loves this quick & easy supper that I've been making for years. It's also great for potlucks. Any leftovers freeze really well.

12-oz. pkg. large elbow
   macaroni, uncooked
1 lb. lean ground beef
1 t. taco seasoning mix
1/4 t. salt
1/4 t. pepper
2 10-oz. cans diced tomatoes
   with green chiles

2 c. pasteurized process cheese,
   cubed
5 slices American cheese
Optional: shredded Cheddar
   cheese

Cook macaroni according to package directions; drain. Meanwhile, in a large, deep skillet over medium heat, cook beef until browned. Drain; stir in taco seasoning, salt and pepper. Add tomatoes with juice and simmer for 5 minutes. Add cubed and sliced cheeses; stir until melted. Add cooked macaroni to beef mixture and stir to coat well. At serving time, top with shredded cheese, if desired. Make 6 servings.

Start a kitchen journal to note favorite recipes and family members' preferences. It'll make meal planning a snap!

Mom's GO-TO *Recipes*

Cheesy Stovetop Potatoes

Cindy Neel
Gooseberry Patch

The key to this dish is slicing the potatoes extra thin. If you don't have a mandoline, just use a sharp knife.

2 T. butter
1/2 c. onion, chopped
1 clove garlic, minced
2 T. all-purpose flour
1 t. salt
1/2 t. garlic powder

1-1/2 c. whole milk, room
   temperature
2 russet potatoes, peeled and
   very thinly sliced
1 c. shredded Cheddar cheese
Garnish: paprika

Melt butter in a Dutch oven over medium heat. Cook onion for 5 minutes, or until softened. Add garlic; cook for one minute. Sprinkle with flour and seasonings; cook and stir until thickened and lightly golden. Gradually whisk in milk; bring to a boil. Layer potatoes in pan. Reduce heat to medium-low; cover and cook for 15 to 20 minutes, until potatoes are fork-tender, stirring often. Add cheese; stir until melted. Dust with paprika. Makes 4 servings.

Easy Tomato-Rice Pilaf

Shirley Howie
Foxboro, MA

This versatile side dish goes well with just about anything!

1 T. olive oil
1/4 c. onion, finely chopped
1 c. long-grain rice, uncooked
14-1/2 oz. can diced tomatoes
   with green pepper, celery
   and onion

1 c. water
1/2 t. dried thyme
salt and pepper to taste

Heat oil in a medium saucepan over medium heat; add onion and rice. Cook, stirring often, until rice is golden, about 5 to 8 minutes. Stir in tomatoes with juice, water and seasonings. Bring to a boil; reduce heat to medium-low. Simmer, tightly covered, until rice is tender, about 18 minutes. Remove from heat. Let stand, covered, for 5 minutes. Fluff rice with a fork before serving. Serves 4.

Skillet & Stovetop SUPPERS

Squash Stir-Fry

Beverley Williams
San Antonio, TX

This side dish is a recipe I tossed together when I was bored with the same old sides. Now it's my most-requested recipe!

2 T. oil	1 t. dried parsley
3 yellow squash, sliced	1/2 t. dried oregano
3 zucchini, sliced	1/2 t. dried thyme
1/4 c. green pepper, diced	1/4 t. garlic powder
1/2 c. chicken broth	Optional: 1 T. cold water,
1 c. tomatoes, diced	1 t. cornstarch

Heat oil in a wok or large skillet over medium heat. Add squash, zucchini and green pepper; cook until tender. Add broth, tomatoes and seasonings; reduce heat to low and simmer for 20 minutes. If a thicker sauce is desired, combine water and cornstarch; stir into mixture and cook until thickened. Makes 6 servings.

Spicy Broccoli Pasta

Mary Beth Schanck
Dothan, AL

I came up with this recipe to get my son to eat vegetables with his much-loved pasta. It makes a really tasty dish!

16-oz. pkg. bowtie pasta, uncooked	1 to 2 T. butter, melted
	red pepper flakes, salt and pepper
1 bunch broccoli, cut into bite-size flowerets	to taste
	Garnish: shredded Parmesan
1/4 c. olive oil	cheese
1/4 c. lemon juice	

Cook pasta according to package instructions, adding broccoli during the last 3 minutes of cooking time. Drain, reserving 1/2 cup cooking liquid. In a large bowl, combine olive oil, lemon juice, butter and seasonings. Add reserved liquid to oil mixture. Add broccoli and cooked pasta; toss to coat well. Serve with Parmesan cheese. Makes 4 servings.

When whipping up a speedy supper, set a kitchen timer...
let it watch the clock and you won't have to!

Mom's GO-TO *Recipes*

Paprika Chicken

Kay Marone
Des Moines, IA

I remember my grandmother serving Paprika Chicken when we came for Sunday dinner, but I never got her recipe. I was happy when I found this recipe...it tastes like hers!

2 T. oil, divided
8 boneless, skinless
   chicken thighs, cut into
   one-inch cubes
1 onion, chopped
2 cloves garlic, minced
1 T. paprika
1/4 t. salt

1/4 t. pepper
14-1/2 oz. can diced tomatoes
2 T. tomato paste
1 green pepper, diced
cooked egg noodles
softened butter to taste
Garnish: sour cream, chopped
   fresh parsley

Heat 1-1/2 tablespoons oil in a large skillet over medium-high heat. Working in batches, add chicken pieces and cook until golden on all sides. Transfer to a plate. Drain and wipe out skillet; add remaining oil. Sauté onion, garlic and seasonings over medium heat, stirring occasionally, for about 5 minutes. Stir in tomatoes with juice and tomato paste. Bring to a boil, stirring and scraping up brown bits from bottom of pan. Reduce heat to medium-low; simmer for 10 minutes. Return chicken and any juices to pan; add green pepper. Cover and simmer for about 10 minutes, until sauce is thick enough to mound on spoon. Toss egg noodles with butter. Serve chicken mixture over buttered egg noodles, garnished as desired. Serves 4.

There is nothing wrong with the world that a sensible woman could not settle in an afternoon.

– Jean Giraudoux

Skillet & Stovetop SUPPERS

Simple Summer Skillet

Courtney Stultz
Weir, KS

There's nothing like fresh garden vegetables to complete a meal. This recipe features a variety of great spring & summer produce that makes a delicious side. Add some cooked bacon or sausage for a heartier all-in-one dish.

1 T. coconut oil or canola oil
1 lb. asparagus spears, cut
  into 1-inch pieces
3 c. fresh kale, spinach or
  mustard greens
2 c. new redskin potatoes, halved

1 c. broccoli, finely chopped
1/2 t. garlic powder
1/2 t. chili powder
1 t. sea salt
1/2 t. pepper

Combine all ingredients in a large skillet over medium heat; stir well. Cook for about 10 to 15 minutes, until tender-crisp, stirring occasionally. Makes 4 servings.

Keep some festive paper plates and napkins tucked away...
they'll set a lighthearted mood on busy evenings,
plus easy clean-up afterward!

Mom's GO-TO *Recipes*

Skillet Enchiladas

Ruth Thomas
Muncie, IN

This easy meal can be ready in 20 minutes! Good on cooler evenings when we're watching football on television. Serve with Spanish rice or refried beans on the side.

1 lb. ground beef
10-oz. can enchilada sauce
10-3/4 oz. can cream of
  mushroom soup
1/3 c. milk
8-oz. pkg. shredded Cheddar
  or Monterey Jack cheese,
  divided

4 to 6 enchilada-size flour
  tortillas
Garnish: chopped avocados,
  diced tomatoes, sour cream

Brown beef in a large skillet over medium heat; drain. Stir in enchilada sauce, soup and milk; simmer until heated through. Meanwhile, spoon 1/4 cup cheese down the center of each tortilla; roll up tortillas and arrange over sauce in skillet. Cover enchiladas with sauce mixture from skillet; top with remaining cheese. Reduce heat to medium-low; simmer for 5 minutes, until cheese is melted. Garnish as desired. Serves 4.

Fix a double batch! Brown 2 pounds of ground beef with 2 packages of taco seasoning mix. Serve half at dinner tonight...freeze the rest for an easy meal of burritos or taco salad another night.

Skillet & Stovetop SUPPERS

Spicy Chicken Skillet

Andrea Heyart
Savannah, TX

*This is one of my favorite go-to recipes on busy nights. Leftover
rotisserie chicken makes this speedy meal even speedier!*

1 to 2 c. cooked chicken, diced
16-oz. jar favorite salsa
1 c. chicken broth

1 c. quick-cooking rice, uncooked
1 c. favorite shredded cheese

In a large skillet over medium heat, combine chicken, salsa and broth.
Bring to a low boil; stir in rice. Cover and simmer over medium-low
heat for 10 minutes. Sprinkle with cheese. Cover and let stand for
another 2 to 3 minutes, until cheese has melted. Serve immediately.
Makes 4 servings.

Hominy Stir-Fry

Pamela DeHart
Roanoke, VA

*My dad and I created this to enjoy on cold days by just tossing some
yummy ingredients together. If you want a little more, add some
diced ham along with the cheese, for an even tastier dish!*

2 T. butter
2 15-1/2 oz. cans hominy,
    drained
1 green pepper, finely chopped

3/4 c. onion, finely chopped
salt and pepper to taste
8-oz. pkg. shredded Colby cheese

Melt butter in a skillet over medium heat. Stir in hominy, green pepper
and onion; season with salt and pepper. Simmer for 5 to 10 minutes,
until onion and pepper are tender; stir. Top with cheese; simmer until
cheese is melted. Stir again before serving. Serves 4.

Mom's GO-TO *Recipes*

Beefy Crunch Skillet

Devi McDonald
Visalia, CA

A delicious one-skillet meal that makes dinner and clean-up a breeze. A great meal idea for busy moms!

2 t. oil
3/4 c. yellow onion, diced
2 lbs. lean ground beef
salt and pepper to taste
10-oz. can diced tomatoes
   with green chiles
15-oz. can tomato sauce
1/2 t. sugar

2 t. chili powder
1/2 t. ground cumin
5 taco-size flour tortillas, cut
   into 1-1/2 inch strips
1/2 c. shredded Cheddar cheese
Garnish: 10 to 12 tortilla chips,
   sour cream, sliced green
   onions

Heat oil in a cast-iron skillet over medium heat. Add onion and sauté for 5 to 6 minutes, until translucent. Add beef; season with salt and pepper. Cook until no pink remains, about 6 to 8 minutes; drain. Add tomatoes with juice and remaining ingredients except garnish; stir to combine. Simmer over medium-low heat for 5 to 6 minutes, until thickened and heated through. Just before serving, crumble tortilla chips over the top. Add a large dollop of sour cream and top with green onions. Makes 6 servings.

Keep the pantry stocked with canned vegetables, creamy soups, rice mixes, pasta and other handy meal-makers. If you pick up 2 or 3 items whenever they're on sale, you'll have a full pantry in no time at all...and you'll always be able to whip up a tasty meal in a jiffy!

Skillet & Stovetop SUPPERS

Simple Sweet-and-Sour Chicken

Mandy Doolittle
Highlands Ranch, CO

This easy meal is ready in about 20 minutes and is a great way to add variety to everyday meals. It's even more delicious if you can use fresh pineapple. Change it up with a pound of uncooked shrimp instead of chicken.

1 tb. olive oil
1 lb. boneless, skinless chicken
    breast, cubed
1/2 c. onion, diced
1 c. red pepper, sliced

1 c. pineapple cubes
10-oz. bottle sweet-and-sour
    sauce
2 c. cooked rice

Heat oil in a skillet over medium heat; add chicken and cook through. Add onion, red pepper and pineapple; mix well. Add sauce; lower heat to medium-low. Simmer for 5 minutes, or until vegetables are crisp-tender. Serve over cooked rice. Makes 4 servings.

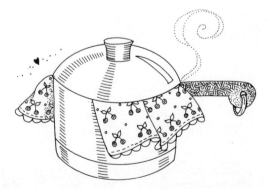

The secret to tender steamed rice! Cook long-cooking rice according to package directions. When it's done, remove pan from heat, cover with a folded tea towel and put the lid back on. Let stand for 5 to 10 minutes before serving. The towel will absorb any excess moisture.

Mom's GO-TO *Recipes*

Cooktop Mac & Cheese

Jodi Spires
Centerville, OH

A fast and easy go-to homemade macaroni & cheese recipe. Creamy and delicious...your family will be asking for this all the time!

8-oz. pkg. elbow macaroni,
  uncooked
2 T. butter
2 eggs, beaten
1/2 t. hot pepper sauce
1/4 t. dry mustard

1 t. kosher salt
1/2 t. pepper
5-oz. can evaporated milk
8-oz. pkg. shredded Cheddar
  cheese

Cook macaroni according to package directions, just until tender. Drain and return to pan; add butter and return to medium-low heat. While macaroni is cooking, whisk together eggs, hot sauce and seasonings in a bowl; set aside. In a small saucepan over medium-high heat, heat milk to almost boiling. Remove from heat. Slowly stir warm milk into egg mixture, one tablespoon at a time. Slowly add egg mixture to cooked macaroni; stir to combine. Add cheese; cook and stir over low heat for 2 to 3 minutes, until slightly thickened and cheese is melted. Makes 6 to 8 servings.

Children will love pasta dishes spooned into individual ramekins or custard cups. Easy to serve and just their size!

Skillet & Stovetop SUPPERS

Tasty Tuna Burgers

Lisa Langston
Conroe, TX

*This is an easy and delish burger...makes for
a nice change from ground beef!*

1 to 2 5-oz. cans tuna, drained
   and flaked
1/2 c. soft bread crumbs
1/2 c. onion, diced
1/2 c. celery, diced
1/3 c. mayonnaise

1 egg, beaten
1 T. olive oil
4 hamburger buns, split
Garnish: lettuce leaves, sliced
   tomato, sliced onion

In a bowl, combine tuna, bread crumbs, onion, celery, mayonnaise and
egg. Shape into 4 patties. Heat olive oil in a skillet over medium heat;
add patties. Cook for 4 to 5 minutes on each side, until lightly golden.
Drain on paper towels. Serve patties in buns with favorite toppings.
Makes 4 servings.

Super-Simple Salmon Patties

Lori Peterson
Effingham, KS

*I grew up on these patties. My mom and grandma used to
make them fairly often and now I make them for my family too!*

14-oz. can salmon, drained
10 to 15 saltine crackers, crushed
2 eggs, beaten
1/4 c. onion, diced

Optional: 1/4 c. green pepper,
   finely chopped
salt and pepper to taste
2 T. canola oil

In a bowl, mash salmon with a fork. Add remaining ingredients except
oil; mix well. If too dry, add another egg; if too wet, add a few more
crackers. Heat oil in a large skillet over medium heat. Cook patties for
2 to 3 minutes per side, until golden. Serves 4.

Tuck burgers into the pockets of halved
pita rounds...easy for small hands to
hold and a tasty change from the
same old hamburger buns.

Mom's GO-TO *Recipes*

One-Pot Spanish Noodles

Carolyn Deckard
Bedford, IN

*This is great to fix on a busy day, so easy! Good for
get-togethers with family & friends.*

6 slices bacon, cut into
   1-inch pieces
1 lb. ground beef
3/4 c. onion, chopped
3/4 c. green pepper, chopped
14-1/2 oz. can diced tomatoes
1-1/2 c. water

1/2 t. dried oregano
red pepper flakes to taste
2 t. salt
1/8 t. pepper
6-oz. pkg. wide egg noodles,
   uncooked

In a skillet over medium heat, cook bacon until crisp. Drain, reserving
drippings in pan; set aside bacon on a paper towel. Sauté beef, onion
and green pepper in reserved drippings; drain. Stir in tomatoes with
juice, water and seasonings; cover and simmer for 10 minutes. Bring to
a full boil and add uncooked noodles, a few at a time. Reduce heat to
medium-low and cover. Simmer for 10 minutes, or until noodles are
tender. Sprinkle with crumbled bacon and serve. Makes 4 to 6 servings.

Onions add so much flavor to simmered dishes. Skip the chopping
(and the tears!)...pick up a few packages of frozen chopped onions.
Add them directly to the skillet, no need to thaw.

Skillet & Stovetop SUPPERS

Ham, Egg & Potato Supper

Lane McLoud
Siloam Springs, AR

I first prepared this one-pan meal many years ago as a newlywed. It is so easy and delicious that it has become a go-to recipe. For variety, add some cooked bacon or sausage...give different cheeses a try. We like the leftovers for breakfast the next day.

1/4 c. green pepper, chopped
1/2 c. onion, chopped
2 T. butter
1 to 2 potatoes, peeled and
    thinly sliced

salt and pepper to taste
1 c. cooked ham, chopped
2 eggs, beaten, room temperature
3/4 c. shredded Cheddar cheese

In a skillet over medium heat, sauté green pepper and onion in butter for 4 minutes. Layer sliced potatoes on top; season with salt and pepper. Cook over medium-low heat for 15 minutes. Sprinkle ham over potatoes; cook another 10 minutes. Pour eggs over ham; cook another 5 to 6 minutes, until eggs are set. Sprinkle cheese on top; cover and let stand until melted. Makes 6 servings.

Just-picked herbs and creamery butter...yum! Blend one cup softened butter with 2 tablespoons fresh parsley, 2 teaspoons fresh oregano and one tablespoon minced garlic. Spread over warm rolls, toss with hot noodles or dollop on steamed veggies...delicious.

Mom's GO-TO *Recipes*

One-Pot Spaghetti

Barb Rudyk
Alberta, Canada

This dish is so flavorful...the spaghetti absorbs the sauce and cooks perfectly. So easy to put to together. Tastes so good with the secret ingredient, chicken broth...and best of all, not much clean-up.

1 lb. ground beef
1 onion, finely diced
1 clove garlic, minced
1 t. Italian seasoning
1 T. dried parsley
14-1/2 oz. can chicken broth

26-oz. jar spaghetti sauce
1/2 c. water
8-oz. pkg. spaghetti, broken
   into pieces
Garnish: grated Parmesan cheese

In a large skillet over medium heat, brown beef and onion. Drain; add garlic and seasonings. Stir in broth, spaghetti sauce and water; bring to a boil. Reduce heat to medium-low; add uncooked spaghetti. Cover and cook for 15 to 20 minutes, until spaghetti is tender, stirring occasionally and adding more water if needed. At serving time, top with Parmesan cheese. Makes 6 servings.

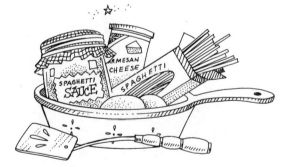

Have a leftovers night once a week! Set out yummy leftovers so everyone can choose their favorite. Add some cookies for dessert...what could be simpler?

Skillet & Stovetop SUPPERS

Zucchini Spaghetti

Kathy Courington
Canton, GA

A different way to use your summer zucchini! It's easy to whip up on a busy night, and very good.

2 c. zucchini, diced
1/2 c. onion, diced
1/4 t. garlic, minced
1 T. olive oil
15-oz. can tomato sauce

1/4 c. water
1/4 c. grated Parmesan cheese
1 t. Italian seasoning
1 t. sugar
2 c. hot cooked spaghetti

In a skillet over medium heat, sauté zucchini, onion and garlic in olive oil for 5 minutes. Add remaining ingredients except spaghetti; mix well to combine. Stir in cooked spaghetti and simmer for 10 minutes, stirring occasionally. Makes 4 to 6 servings.

There's a trick to measuring just enough spaghetti for cooking.
Check your spaghetti server...if it has a quarter-size hole in it,
that's a 2-ounce measure, just enough for one serving.
No more wasted spaghetti!

Mom's GO-TO *Recipes*

Easy Skillet Pork & Onions
Mary Ann Constanzer
South China, ME

The beauty of this recipe is two-fold...its ease and its flavor. These pork chops will fall apart, with no knife needed! Serve with cooked rice, noodles or mashed potatoes. Any leftovers are delicious on a slice of bread in the lunchbox the next day.

1 c. all-purpose flour
garlic powder to taste
3 to 4-lb. boneless pork rib roast,
    cut into one-inch-thick
    pork chops

1 to 2 T. oil
3 to 4 10-1/2 oz. cans French
    onion soup, divided

Combine flour and garlic powder in a shallow dish. Dredge pork chops in mixture. In a large heavy skillet, brown chops in oil on both sides. Pour 3 cans of soup over chops. Cover and simmer over medium-low heat for 2 hours, turning occasionally to prevent sticking. If needed, add remaining can of soup. Makes 6 servings.

Quick Southern-Style Green Beans
Beth Bennett
Stratham, NH

One night, I needed a side dish for dinner, but there was no time for slow-simmered southern green beans. This is what I came up with...it was surprisingly good!

1 lb. fresh green beans, trimmed
1/4 c. butter
2 to 3 T. bacon bits

1 to 2 t. Creole seasoning,
    to taste

Cover beans with water in a saucepan. Cook over medium heat until fork-tender. Drain well; add butter and stir gently until melted. Add bacon bits and seasoning; stir again. Cover and let stand for 15 minutes. Stir and serve. Makes 4 servings.

Skillet & Stovetop SUPPERS

Garlic-Herb Skillet Potatoes

Jennie Gist
Gooseberry Patch

An easy and delicious potato dish...it makes a nice change!
You don't even need to peel the potatoes.

1 T. butter
1 T. olive oil
4 russet potatoes, thinly sliced
1 t. dried rosemary
1 t. dried thyme

1 t. dried oregano
1 t. dried parsley
1/4 t. paprika
salt and pepper to taste
1 to 1-1/2 T. garlic, minced

In a large skillet over medium heat, melt butter with olive oil. Arrange potato slices in skillet in a single layer. Cook without stirring for 5 minutes, or until potatoes are lightly golden on the bottom. Sprinkle with seasonings; turn potatoes over. Continue cooking for 5 minutes, or until tender. Sprinkle with garlic; toss lightly for one minute, or until garlic has softened. Makes 4 servings.

Lemony iced tea is so refreshing with meals. Brew 9 tea bags in 3 quarts boiling water for 5 minutes. Discard tea bags, then stir in a 12-ounce can of frozen lemonade concentrate and a cup of sugar. Chill; serve over ice cubes.

Mom's GO-TO *Recipes*

Pan-Fried Chicken Thighs

Jo Ann
Gooseberry Patch

My family loves this tender, golden chicken. I've come to prefer chicken thighs over boneless chicken breasts, as they're so much more flavorful...cheaper too! Serve with mashed potatoes.

1 yellow onion, chopped
4 cloves garlic, minced
8 sprigs fresh thyme
1/2 t. salt

1/2 t. pepper
3 T. olive oil, divided
6 to 8 chicken thighs

In a large bowl, combine onion, garlic, thyme, salt and pepper. Stir in one tablespoon oil; add chicken and turn to coat well. Heat remaining oil in a large heavy skillet over medium heat for 2 minutes. Add chicken to skillet, skin-side down. Spoon onion mixture in bowl over chicken. Cook for 10 minutes, stirring occasionally. Turn chicken over; stir mixture in skillet. Cook another 5 to 6 minutes, until chicken juices run clear when pierced. Makes 6 to 8 servings.

Skillet gravy is easy to make. Melt a tablespoon of butter in a skillet over medium heat. Sprinkle in a tablespoon of flour and whisk for one minute. Add a cup of chicken or beef broth and a dash of pepper. Stir well, lower heat and simmer for about 5 minutes, until gravy is thickened.

Skillet & Stovetop SUPPERS

Smoky-Sweet Potato Spirals

Courtney Stultz
Weir, KS

*We love using a vegetable spiralizer to change up our dinner plates.
Sometimes just changing the look of a vegetable makes it more
appealing to my family! This recipe cooks up fast and is loaded
with flavor.*

1 T. oil
3 to 4 sweet potatoes, peeled
    and spiral-cut
1/2 c. onion, sliced
1 clove garlic, minced
1/2 t. chili powder

1/2 t. ground cumin
1 t. salt
1/2 t. pepper
1/4 t. smoke-flavored cooking
    sauce

Heat oil in a large skillet over medium heat. Add sweet potato spirals,
onion and garlic. Sprinkle with remaining ingredients. Cook over
medium heat for about 15 to 20 minutes, until tender, tossing a few
times while cooking. Serves 4.

Add extra texture to fresh veggies of all kinds...use a spiral slicer or
a crinkle cutter to cut them into slices and sticks.

Mom's GO-TO *Recipes*

Kay's Mexican Dish

Lynda Bolton
East Peoria, IL

Years ago, my husband's cousin shared this recipe with me and it quickly became one of our kids' favorite meals. It reheats beautifully, which is great for lunch, and can be made mild or with more heat, for those wanting more of a burn!

1 lb. ground beef
1/2 c. onion, diced
1/4 t. seasoning blend with
 onion and garlic
1/8 t. salt
1/8 t. pepper
15-oz. can mild or hot chili,
 no beans
15-1/2 oz. can mild or hot
 chili beans
10-3/4 oz. can Cheddar
 cheese soup

8-oz. jar mild or hot
 taco sauce
1/2 c. mild or hot salsa
Optional: 14-1/2 oz. can diced
 tomatoes, drained
13-oz. pkg. nacho-flavored
 tortilla chips
Garnish: shredded Cheddar
 or Mexican-blend cheese,
 shredded lettuce,
 diced tomato

Brown beef with onion in a large skillet, breaking up beef; drain. Wipe out skillet with a paper towel; return beef mixture to skillet. Stir in seasonings. Add chili, beans, soup, taco sauce, salsa and tomatoes, if using. Stir well; simmer over medium-low heat for 15 to 20 minutes, until heated through. To serve, place a handful of chips on each plate. Spoon beef mixture over chips; add desired toppings. Eat with your fingers (have plenty of napkins on hand!) and spoon up the rest. Makes 4 to 6 servings.

Pick up a dozen pint-size Mason jars...they're fun and practical for serving ice-cold lemonade, sweet tea or frosty root beer at casual meals!

Classic
Oven-Baked
COMFORT FOODS

Mom's GO-TO *Recipes*

Italian Chicken, Green Beans & Potatoes

Bethany Hendrix
Springfield, MO

My mom used to make this one-dish dinner for us when we were little! Whenever I make it myself, it's like I'm taking a trip down memory lane.

3 to 4 chicken breasts, cut in half
8 to 10 new redskin potatoes,
   cut into quarters
2 c. fresh or canned green beans

1-oz. pkg. Italian salad dressing
   mix
1/4 c. butter, melted

Arrange chicken in the center of a greased 13"x9" baking pan. Place potatoes on one side of chicken; place beans on the other side. Sprinkle salad dressing mix over everything; drizzle with melted butter. Cover with aluminum foil. Bake at 350 degrees for about one hour, until chicken juices run clear when pierced. Makes 4 to 6 servings.

Making dinner in the oven tonight? Set the oven to the right temperature before you begin prepping ingredients. By the time the dish is ready, the oven will be preheated and ready to go.

Classic Oven-Baked
COMFORT FOODS

Mom's Pizza-Style Spaghetti

Kelly Thomas
Sarver, PA

*My favorite meal as a kid! I make this meal often for my own family.
It reheats really well...just add a little more spaghetti sauce and it
is wonderful. My daughter loves helping me make this.*

16-oz. pkg. thin spaghetti,
   uncooked
2 eggs, beaten
1 c. milk

2 15-1/2 oz. jars spaghetti sauce
1-1/2 c. thinly sliced pepperoni
2 to 4 c. shredded mozzarella
   cheese

Cook spaghetti according to package directions; drain. In a large bowl,
whisk together eggs and milk; pour over spaghetti and toss well. Spread
spaghetti mixture in a greased 18"x11" jelly-roll pan. Top with spaghetti
sauce. Arrange pepperoni slices in rows over the sauce; sprinkle with
desired amount of cheese. Bake at 350 degrees for 30 minutes. Let
stand 5 minutes; cut into squares. Serves 8 to 10.

Easy Cheesy Breadsticks

Lynn Williams
Muncie, IN

Jazz up a tube of pizza dough in just a few minutes!

10-oz. tube refrigerated pizza
   crust
1 T. butter, melted
1/2 c. shredded Provolone cheese

1 T. grated Parmesan cheese
1 T. dried basil
1/4 t. garlic salt
Optional: warm marinara sauce

Unroll pizza dough onto a greased baking sheet. Brush dough with
butter; sprinkle evenly with cheeses and spices. With a pizza cutter cut
dough lengthwise into 12 strips. Cut strips in half to make 24 strips;
do not separate strips. Bake at 425 degrees for 10 to 12 minutes, until
lightly golden. Recut along each strip before removing from baking
sheet. Serve with warm marinara sauce, if desired. Makes 2 dozen.

Mom's GO-TO *Recipes*

Quick Taco Bake

Carolyn Deckard
Bedford, IN

This has always been one of my kids' favorite dishes. They are all married now with families of their own, and they fix this quick meal often. We use our homemade salsa from our garden.

1 lb. ground beef
10-3/4 oz. can tomato soup
1 c. thick chunky salsa or
   picante sauce
1/2 c. milk

6 8-inch flour tortillas, cut into
   1-inch squares
1 c. shredded Cheddar cheese,
   divided

In a large skillet over medium-high heat, cook beef until browned; drain. Stir in soup, salsa, milk, tortilla pieces and half of the cheese. Spoon into a lightly greased 2-quart shallow casserole dish. Cover and bake at 400 degrees for 30 minutes, or until hot and bubbly. Sprinkle with remaining cheese. Makes 4 servings.

Oven-Baked Meatballs

Melanie Lively
Oliver Springs, TN

I always keep a batch of these meatballs on hand. Once baked, freeze half to use later...a real time-saver! They're great in marinara sauce for spaghetti or meatball subs. You can also warm them in barbecue sauce or chili sauce as cocktail meatball appetizers. They're even great in stroganoff sauce on hot buttered egg noodles!

2 lbs. ground beef
1-1/2 c. soft bread crumbs
1/2 c. milk

1/4 c. onion, finely chopped
2 eggs, beaten
1-1/2 t. salt

In a large bowl, combine all ingredients. Mix well; shape into one-inch balls. Place meatballs on ungreased rimmed baking sheets. Bake at 375 degrees for 25 to 30 minutes, until no longer pink in the center. Serves 8.

Dip your hands into cold water before shaping meatballs...
the meat won't stick to your hands.

Classic Oven-Baked
COMFORT FOODS

Zucchini with Cheese

Sharon Matheisen
Scio, OR

An easy way to use up zucchini...even the kids will love it!

1/4 c. all-purpose flour
1-1/2 t. dried oregano, divided
1-1/2 t. salt, divided
1/4 t. pepper, divided
1-1/2 lbs. zucchini, sliced
　　1/4-inch thick

1/4 c. olive oil
2 to 3 ripe tomatoes, sliced
1 c. sour cream
1/2 c. grated Parmesan cheese

In a large bowl, combine flour, 1/2 teaspoon oregano, 1/2 teaspoon salt and 1/8 teaspoon pepper. Toss zucchini slices in flour mixture, coating well; set aside. Heat oil in a large skillet over medium heat. Sauté zucchini until golden, about 4 minutes per side. Layer zucchini in a lightly greased 8"x8" baking pan; top with tomato slices. Combine sour cream and remaining seasonings; spread evenly over tomatoes. Sprinkle with Parmesan cheese. Bake, uncovered, at 350 degrees for 30 to 35 minutes, until cheese is melted and zucchini is tender. Makes 6 servings.

Try crushed tortilla chips as a crunchy casserole topping. They come in so many varieties like Cheddar cheese, ranch and spicy chili...there's sure to be one that's a hit with your family!

Mom's GO-TO *Recipes*

Anytime Casserole Potatoes

Kathleen Kennedy
Port Angeles, WA

My whole family loves my casserole potatoes! This is a tried & true recipe whenever I'm using up leftover meats and vegetables. The ham can be changed to chicken or ground beef...asparagus changed to frozen peas or corn. With cream-of-something soup and shredded cheese, it's quick & easy to make.

6 potatoes, peeled and sliced
6 thin spears asparagus, trimmed
   and sliced
10-3/4 oz. can cream of
   mushroom or celery soup
1/2 to 3/4 c. milk

3/4 lb. cooked ham steak, diced
salt and pepper to taste
8-oz. pkg. shredded Cheddar or
   Colby-Jack cheese, divided
1 to 2 green onions, sliced

Cover potatoes with water in a saucepan. Boil over medium-high heat until nearly fork-tender. Drain; set aside. Meanwhile, bring a separate saucepan of water to a boil; add asparagus. Cook for 2 minutes; drain and set aside. In a bowl, whisk together soup and milk. Spread a greased 9"x9" baking pan with just enough soup mixture to lightly cover bottom of pan. Layer with half each of potatoes, asparagus, ham and a little salt and pepper; add 1/3 each of remaining sauce and cheese. Repeat layering, ending with a layer of sauce and cheese. Top with onions. Cover and bake at 350 degrees for 40 to 45 minutes, until hot and bubbly. Makes 6 to 8 servings.

Before covering a cheese-topped dish with aluminum foil, spray the foil with non-stick vegetable spray. The cheese won't stick to the foil!

94

Classic Oven-Baked COMFORT FOODS

Roasted Tomato Cavatappi

Jo Ann
Gooseberry Patch

This is a yummy fresh side or meatless main that's perfect after you've come back from the farmers' market. If you can't find curly cavatappi pasta, use rotini or penne pasta.

8-oz. pkg. cavatappi pasta,
  uncooked
1/2 c. boiling water
1 T. olive oil
1 cube chicken bouillon

2 cloves garlic, minced
8 roma tomatoes, quartered
1 medium onion, cut into wedges
1/4 c. fresh basil, chopped
Garnish: grated Parmesan cheese

Cook pasta according to package directions; drain. Meanwhile, combine boiling water, oil, bouillon cube and garlic; let stand until bouillon dissolves. In an ungreased shallow 13"x9" baking pan, combine tomatoes, onion and bouillon mixture; stir gently. Bake, uncovered, at 400 degrees for 30 minutes, or until tomatoes and onion are tender, stirring occasionally. Toss tomato mixture with hot pasta and basil. Garnish with Parmesan cheese. Makes 4 to 6 servings.

The most indispensable ingredient of all good home cooking...
love, for those you are cooking for.

– Sophia Loren

Mom's GO-TO *Recipes*

Church Dinner Chicken

Diane Himpelmann
Ringwood, IL

This chicken dish has been a family favorite in our home for over 40 years. It is my husband's favorite meal! Make two pans if you are having company. If there are any leftovers, I dice the chicken and fry with the rice in a pan, adding a cup of frozen peas.

3-lb. frying chicken, cut up,
   or 4 chicken breasts
Optional: all-purpose flour
1/2 c. butter
3/4 c. onion, chopped

3 c. water
4 cubes chicken bouillon
1-1/2 c. long-cooking rice,
   uncooked

Coat chicken pieces with flour, if skinless. Melt butter in a large skillet over medium heat; cook chicken until golden on all sides. Remove chicken to a plate, reserving drippings in skillet. Brown onion in drippings; stir in water and bouillon cubes. Bring to a boil; stir until bouillon is dissolved and remove from heat. Sprinkle uncooked rice in a greased 13"x9" baking pan; arrange chicken pieces on top. Spoon onion mixture over chicken. Cover with aluminum foil. Bake at 350 degrees for 2 hours, or until chicken and rice are tender. Serves 4 to 6.

Brown Sugar Nut Muffins

Beckie Apple
Grannis, AR

These muffins are so moist and are delicious anytime. It takes only minutes to mix and bake a batch. They are wonderful split and slathered with butter or honey.

2 eggs, beaten
1/2 c. butter, melted
1 t. vanilla extract

1 c. brown sugar, packed
3/4 c. self-rising flour
1/2 c. pecans, finely chopped

In a large bowl, whisk eggs into melted butter; add vanilla and mix well. Add remaining ingredients; mix just until moistened. Spoon batter into paper-lined muffin cups, filling 3/4 full. Bake at 375 degrees for 8 to 10 minutes. Makes about one dozen.

Classic Oven-Baked
COMFORT FOODS

Chicken Cashew Casserole

Annette Ceravolo
Hoover, AL

My neighbor made this dish for us when my daughter was born, 30 years ago. I've added my own touches over the years and my family loves it. I like to serve it with a tossed salad and steamed veggies.

1 c. cooked chicken, diced
10-3/4 oz. can cream of
    mushroom or celery soup
1 c. celery, diced
1/2 c. onion, diced

1/2 c. chopped cashews
1/4 c. chicken broth
salt and pepper to taste
3-oz. can chow mein noodles,
    divided

In a large bowl, combine all ingredients, reserving half of the noodles. Mix lightly and spoon into a greased 2-quart casserole dish. Sprinkle reserved noodles on top. Bake, uncovered, at 325 degrees for 30 minutes, or until hot and bubbly. Makes 4 servings.

For the juiciest chicken, try poaching. Cover boneless, skinless chicken breasts with water in a saucepan. Bring to a boil, then turn down the heat. Cover and simmer over low heat for 10 to 12 minutes, until chicken is no longer pink in the center. Allow to cool in the broth before using.

Mom's GO-TO *Recipes*

Baked Chicken & Rice with Black Beans

Shirley Howie
Foxboro, MA

*This is an easy one-dish meal that I make often. For variety,
I sometimes substitute Monterey Jack or Mexican-blend cheese for
the Cheddar cheese. It's fun to experiment and always very tasty!*

10-oz. pkg. yellow rice mix,
   uncooked
1 c. onion, diced
1/2 c. green pepper, diced
1/2 c. carrot, peeled and diced
1 T. olive oil

2 c. cooked chicken, cubed
15-oz. can black beans, drained
10-oz. can diced tomatoes with
   green chiles
8-oz. pkg. shredded Cheddar
   cheese, divided

Cook rice according to package directions; set aside. Meanwhile, in a
skillet over medium heat, sauté onion, green pepper and carrot in oil
for 10 minutes, or until tender. In a large bowl, combine cooked rice,
onion mixture, chicken, black beans, tomatoes with juice and
1-1/2 cups cheese. Spoon into a lightly greased 13"x9" baking pan;
sprinkle with remaining cheese. Cover and bake at 350 degrees for
30 minutes. Uncover and bake another 10 minutes, or until cheese is
melted. Serves 6.

Take it easy on alternate Friday nights...arrange for a friendly
dinner swap! One week, you make a double batch of a favorite
casserole and deliver one to a friend. Next week, she returns
the favor. You're sure to discover some great new recipes
while gaining a little free time too.

Classic Oven-Baked
COMFORT FOODS

Down-Home Texas Chicken & Peppers

Janet Dolbow
West Deptford, NJ

My whole family loves this recipe! A nearby diner used to make a dish like this, but they stopped serving it, so I decided to make it on my own. I like mine better than theirs! And it's not hard to make.

1 to 2 lbs. boneless, skinless
   chicken tenders, cut into
   bite-size pieces
2 T. olive oil, divided
3 red peppers, sliced
3 yellow peppers, sliced
3 orange peppers, sliced

2 onions, chopped
18-oz. bottle barbecue sauce
16-oz. pkg. shredded mild
   Cheddar cheese
8-oz. pkg. shredded mozzarella
   cheese

In a large skillet over medium heat, cook chicken in one tablespoon olive oil; remove from heat. Meanwhile, in a separate large skillet, sauté peppers and onions in remaining oil until peppers are soft and onion is translucent. Drain vegetables on paper towels. Spread some of the barbecue sauce in the bottom of a lightly greased 13"x9" glass baking pan; arrange chicken and pepper mixture over the sauce. Top with remaining barbecue sauce; top with cheeses. Bake, uncovered, at 350 degrees for about 20 to 30 minutes, until heated through and cheese is melted. Let stand about 10 minutes before serving. Makes 8 servings.

Create a meal plan for the week, including all of your favorite quick & easy meals...spaghetti on Monday, tacos on Tuesday and so forth. Post it on the fridge along with a shopping list. No more last-minute scrambles for dinner!

Mom's GO-TO *Recipes*

Leona's Imperial Chicken

Leona Krivda
Belle Vernon, PA

We have been enjoying this recipe at our house for many years. It is the first recipe both of my daughters made on their own when they made their first dinner for us. It is a quick & easy, very good recipe. Hope you all enjoy it as much as we do.

1 c. grated Parmesan cheese
1 c. Italian-flavored dry bread
   crumbs
1 T. dried parsley
1/4 t. garlic powder

3/4 t. salt
1/2 t. pepper
8 boneless, skinless chicken
   breasts
1/2 c. butter, melted

In a shallow dish, combine all ingredients except chicken and butter; set aside. Pound chicken to flatten. Dip chicken into butter; roll in crumb mixture to coat well. Arrange chicken in a lightly greased 13"x9" baking pan. Drizzle any remaining butter over chicken. Bake, uncovered, at 350 degrees for 50 to 60 minutes, until golden and chicken juices run clear. Makes 8 servings.

Parmesan Baked Potatoes

Hope Davenport
Portland, TX

These tasty potatoes are a nice change from ordinary baked potatoes.

6 T. butter, melted
1/4 c. grated Parmesan cheese

6 redskin or russet potatoes,
   halved lengthwise

Spread butter in a 13"x9" baking pan or a rimmed baking sheet. Sprinkle cheese over butter; arrange potatoes cut-side down in pan. Bake at 400 degrees for 40 to 45 minutes, until fork-tender. Serves 6.

Why not bake some extra potatoes?
You can grate them and dice them for
hashbrowns or soups, slice them for home
fries or whip up a quick potato salad.

Classic Oven-Baked
COMFORT FOODS

Shirley's So-Easy Pork Chops

Shirley Howie
Foxboro, MA

This is one of my favorite ways to prepare pork chops. They are quick & easy to make and are always yummy! For variety, I sometimes use thyme, basil and other seasonings that I have in my cupboard.

1 c. Italian-flavored dry bread
   crumbs
1/4 c. grated Parmesan cheese
1 T. dried oregano
1-1/2 t. dried sage

1 t. dried rosemary
1/4 t. salt
1 t. pepper
4 pork chops
1/4 c. butter, melted

In a shallow bowl, combine all ingredients except pork chops and butter; mix well. Dip pork chops into melted butter and then into bread crumb mixture; coat thoroughly. Arrange pork chops in a lightly greased 13"x9" baking pan in a single layer. Bake, uncovered, at 375 degrees for 35 to 40 minutes, until no longer pink in the center. Makes 4 servings.

For a tasty change, coat pork chops with grainy mustard and dredge them in finely ground pretzels before baking.

Mom's GO-TO Recipes

Boys' Favorite Mac & Cheese

Andrea Vernon
Logansport, IN

This is a family favorite...it has made an appearance at many family gatherings! A friend gave me the basic recipe for this years ago and I have changed it up a bit. It may seem like a lot of cheese for the amount of pasta, but trust me on the amounts! May be made one day ahead and then baked.

2 c. elbow macaroni, uncooked
8-oz. pkg. shredded Cheddar or
   Co-Jack cheese
1 c. cottage cheese
1 c. sour cream
1 c. whole or 2% milk
1 egg, beaten
2 t. seasoned salt or Cajun
   seasoned salt
1 t. paprika

Cook macaroni according to package directions, just until tender; drain. Meanwhile, combine cheeses, sour cream, milk, egg and salt in a large bowl. Add cooked macaroni; stir gently to coat well. Transfer to an ungreased 13"x9" baking pan; sprinkle with paprika. Cover with greased aluminum foil. Bake at 350 degrees for 30 minutes. Uncover; bake for an additional 30 minutes, or until bubbly and golden. Makes 8 to 10 servings.

Variations:

• Add diced ham or chicken to make it a main dish

• For a flavor change, add one can of diced green chiles

• Swap in some Swiss cheese or Gouda for a flavor change

If you like to shred your own cheese, place the wrapped cheese in the freezer for 10 to 20 minutes...it will glide right across the grater!

Classic Oven-Baked
COMFORT FOODS

Baked Zucchini

Tina Fox
Lake Arrowhead, CA

My family loves zucchini, so I am always creating new zucchini recipes. This is a great side dish that my family just loves. I make my own marinara sauce, but store-bought sauce is fine too. My family loves it with homemade ranch dressing.

5 to 6 zucchini, ends trimmed
    and cut into thick matchsticks
kosher salt to taste
1 c. all-purpose flour
2 eggs, beaten
1/4 c. whole milk
2 c. panko bread crumbs
1 c. grated Parmesan cheese,
    divided
olive oil to taste
pepper to taste
Garnish: warm marinara sauce

In a shallow bowl, season zucchini with salt; sprinkle with flour and toss to coat. Whisk eggs with milk in a small bowl. In another bowl, combine panko crumbs and 1/2 cup Parmesan cheese. Working in batches, dip each piece of zucchini into egg mixture, letting excess drip off; coat in panko mixture and arrange on a parchment paper-lined baking sheet. Drizzle with olive oil; sprinkle with pepper and remaining Parmesan cheese. Bake at 425 degrees for 18 to 20 minutes, until tender and golden. Serve with marinara sauce on the side for dipping. Makes 8 servings.

Need to clean baked-on food from a casserole dish? Place a dryer sheet in the dish and fill with warm water. Let the dish stand overnight, then sponge clean. You'll find the fabric softener will really soften the baked-on food.

Mom's GO-TO *Recipes*

Southwest Pork Tenderloin with Vegetables

Sandra Mirando
Depew, NY

*I have shared this recipe with so many of my friends
and coworkers...everyone loves it!*

1-1/2 lb. pork tenderloin
4 baking potatoes, quartered
4 red and/or orange peppers,
   thickly sliced

1 onion, sliced
1/4 c. oil
1-1/4 oz. pkg taco seasoning mix
Optional: salsa, sour cream

Combine pork, potatoes, peppers, onion, oil and seasoning mix in a
large bowl; mix to coat. Place pork in the center of an aluminum foil-
lined rimmed baking sheet; arrange vegetables around pork. Bake at
400 degrees for 40 to 45 minutes, until pork and potatoes are tender.
Let stand several minutes before slicing pork. Garnish with salsa and
sour cream if desired. Serves 4 to 6.

Vintage enamelware dishpans are so useful in the kitchen...don't
pass them by at tag sales! They're perfect for mixing up company-
size batches of salad, dressing and so much more, even for
serving popcorn on family movie night.

Classic Oven-Baked
COMFORT FOODS

Sheet Pan Sausage Bake

Sarah Oravecz
Gooseberry Patch

This one-pan dinner is super-easy and delicious! Any kind of uncooked sausage can be used. If you prefer, use quartered potatoes instead of fennel bulbs. Either way, it's a winner.

4 to 6 bratwurst sausage links
1 lb. assorted baby sweet
   peppers, halved
1 red onion, cut into one-inch
   chunks

2 fennel bulbs, cored and cut
   into one-inch chunks
1 T. olive oil
salt and pepper to taste

Pierce each sausage several times with a knife tip. Arrange on a parchment paper-lined rimmed baking sheet and set aside. Combine peppers, onion and fennel in a large bowl; drizzle with oil. Season generously with salt and pepper; toss to coat. Arrange vegetables around sausages in a single layer. Bake at 375 degrees for 40 to 45 minutes, turning sausages and vegetables once, until sausages are cooked through and vegetables are tender. Makes 4 to 6 servings.

Create your own all-in-one dinner on a baking sheet by combining recipes...for example, a pork chop recipe and one for broccoli. If the recipes call for different oven temperatures, go with the one for the meat. Watch closely, removing the veggie to a plate if it's done more quickly. One less pan to wash!

Mom's GO-TO *Recipes*

Chile Mañana

Margaret Lynn Lind
Deming, NM

Chile mañana literally means "chile tomorrow," but no one really knows how this got its name! It's been in my family since the 1960s. This dish may be prepared ahead of time and refrigerated, then baked mañana. Serve with warm flour tortillas and a simple chopped salad of lettuce and tomatoes. It's easy to make and easily doubled.

1 lb. ground beef
3/4 c. onion, chopped
salt and pepper to taste
Optional: 1/2 t. garlic powder
10-3/4 oz. can cream of
   mushroom soup

3/4 c. milk
4-oz. can mild diced green chiles,
   drained
6 to 8 corn tortillas
1 to 2 c. shredded Cheddar
   cheese

In a skillet over medium heat, brown beef with onion. Drain; sprinkle with seasonings as desired. Stir in soup, milk and chiles; set aside. Arrange 3 to 4 tortillas in the bottom of a lightly greased 13"x9" baking pan, tearing to fit as needed. Layer with half of the beef mixture; sprinkle with half of cheese. Repeat layers. Bake, uncovered, at 350 degrees for 25 to 30 minutes, until hot, bubbly and cheese is melted. Serves 4.

Southern Cornbread

Mary Shearer
Winchester, KY

This recipe has been in my family for many years. It's always a big hit at family dinners!

3 eggs, beaten
1/3 c. oil
8-oz. container sour cream

14-3/4 oz. can creamed corn
1 c. self-rising cornmeal

In a large bowl, combine all ingredients. Mix well until batter is moistened. Pour batter into a hot greased cast-iron skillet. Bake at 425 degrees for 20 minutes, or until golden. Cut into wedges to serve. Makes 6 to 8 servings.

Classic Oven-Baked COMFORT FOODS

Taco Pie

Hadley Thomas
Frankfort, IN

This recipe is a quick family favorite at our house...the kids and grown-ups all love it! It comes together quickly, and that makes it an easy, quick warm meal on a busy night.

1 lb. ground beef
1/2 c. onion, diced
1/3 c. water
1-oz. pkg. taco seasoning mix
1/2 c. canned refried beans
8-oz. tube refrigerated crescent
   rolls, separated

1-1/2 c. taco-flavored tortilla
   chips, crushed and divided
1 c. sour cream
1-1/2 c. shredded Cheddar
   cheese
Garnish: shredded lettuce,
   diced tomatoes

Brown beef with onion in a skillet over medium heat; drain. Stir in water and taco seasoning; cook until slightly thickened. Stir in beans; remove from heat. Press crescent rolls into a 9" pie plate to form a crust. Sprinkle one cup of crushed tortilla chips into crust; spoon beef mixture into crust. Spread sour cream over top; sprinkle with cheese. Bake at 350 degrees for 20 minutes, until crust is golden and cheese is melted. Remove from oven; let rest 10 minutes. Serve topped with lettuce, tomato and additional crushed chips. Makes 8 to 10 servings.

Mom's best recipes usually make lots of servings, perfect for sharing. Invite a neighbor or a co-worker that you'd like to get to know better...encourage your kids to invite a friend. You're sure to have a great time together!

Mom's GO-TO *Recipes*

Panko-Crusted Fish Sticks

Cheri Maxwell
Gulf Breeze, FL

My kids like any kind of fish sticks. These are tasty enough for us adults to enjoy too!

1 egg, lightly beaten
salt and pepper to taste
2 c. panko bread crumbs
2 T. olive oil
1 T. seafood seasoning

1-1/2 lbs. tilapia fillets,
   cut into wide strips
Garnish: tartar sauce,
   lemon wedges

Whisk egg with salt and pepper in a shallow bowl. In another bowl, combine panko crumbs, oil and seasoning. Dip fish fillets into egg, shaking off excess, then into panko mixture, pressing to coat well. Place fish fillets on aluminum foil-lined baking sheets. Bake at 475 degrees for 12 to 15 minutes, turning baking sheets halfway through, until lightly golden. Garnish as desired. Makes 4 to 6 servings.

Roasted Broccoli

Donna Riley
Browns Summit, NC

My daughter Kimberly taught me this recipe. I love that she can teach me new things!

1 to 2 bunches broccoli, cut into
   2-inch flowerets

2 to 3 T. olive oil
garlic salt to taste

Arrange broccoli on an aluminum foil-lined baking sheet. Drizzle with olive oil; sprinkle generously with garlic salt. Toss to coat all pieces; spread into a single layer. Bake at 400 degrees for 30 minutes, or until tender and lightly charred, stirring after 15 minutes. Serve immediately. Makes 6 to 8 servings.

Classic Oven-Baked
COMFORT FOODS

Baked Parmesan Chicken Strips

Holly Child
Parker, CO

I use this recipe whenever I need a quick dinner for my family. Everyone loves it and there are never any leftovers! Serve with favorite dipping sauces, or with pasta and salad on the side.

10 chicken tenders, thawed
   if frozen
1 c. all-purpose flour
1 t. salt
1 t. pepper

2 eggs, beaten
1 T. water
1 c. dry bread crumbs
1 c. shredded Parmesan cheese

Pat chicken tenders dry with a paper towel; set aside. Combine flour, salt and pepper in a shallow bowl; in a second shallow bowl whisk together eggs and water. Combine bread crumbs and Parmesan cheese in another bowl. Coat each chicken tender in flour mixture; dip into egg mixture, coating completely and dip into bread crumb mixture. Place coated chicken tenders on a greased baking sheet. Bake at 425 degrees for 15 minutes. Turn over; bake for an additional 5 minutes, or until crisp and golden. Makes 4 to 6 servings.

Make a delicious honey-mustard dip for chicken nuggets with 2/3 cup honey and 1/3 cup mustard. Try different kinds of honey and mustard to create flavor variations.

Mom's GO-TO *Recipes*

Inside-Out Chicken Enchiladas

Becky Butler
Keller, TX

My son had suggested creamy chicken enchiladas for supper, but I was pressed for time. So I came up with a shortcut we all love! I make the filling and sauce together, then we assemble them like tacos right at the dinner table. Same great taste, but easier and quicker to prepare than enchiladas!

3 boneless, skinless chicken
    breasts, cut into 3 to 4 strips
1-1/2 T. fajita or grill seasoning
10-3/4 oz. can cream of chicken
    soup
2 T. canned mild chopped
    green chiles

8-oz. container sour cream
1 t. pepper, or to taste
1-1/2 c. shredded Mexican-
    cheese blend
10 to 12 enchilada-size corn
    tortillas

In a large plastic zipping bag, toss chicken strips with seasoning. Grill or sauté chicken over medium-high heat until chicken is no longer pink inside. Arrange chicken strips in a 9"x9" baking pan coated in non-stick vegetable spray; set aside. In a bowl, stir together soup, chiles, sour cream and pepper. Spoon soup mixture over chicken strips; top evenly with cheese. Bake, uncovered, at 350 degrees for 20 to 25 minutes, until cheese is melted and sauce is bubbly around the edges. Meanwhile, heat tortillas on both sides in a heavy, dry skillet over medium-high heat. Keep warm in aluminum foil. Serve chicken mixture and warm tortillas at the dinner table. Fill each tortilla with one to 2 chicken strips, sauce and melted cheese. Makes 5 to 6 servings.

A speedy side for any south-of-the-border supper! Stir spicy salsa and shredded Mexican-blend cheese into hot cooked rice. Cover and let stand a few minutes, until the cheese melts.

Classic Oven-Baked
COMFORT FOODS

Beefy Bean & Corn Casserole

Katherine Harrison
Goodwater, AL

A favorite Monday dinner after a long weekend...
my husband loves this!

1-1/2 lbs. ground beef
1 onion, chopped
3/4 c. green pepper, chopped
15-1/2 oz. can chili beans in
    mild chili sauce
15-3/4 oz. can sweet corn &
    diced peppers, drained

14-1/2 oz. can diced tomatoes
    with green chiles, drained
1 c. barbecue sauce
1/2 t. salt
1/2 t. pepper
8-1/2 oz. pkg. corn muffin mix

In a skillet over medium heat, brown beef with onion and green pepper; drain. Stir in remaining ingredients except corn muffin mix. Transfer to a lightly greased 13"x9" baking pan; set aside. Prepare corn muffin mix according to package directions; spoon batter over beef mixture. Bake at 400 degrees for 20 to 30 minutes, until beef mixture is bubbly and topping is golden. Makes 6 servings.

For a quick & tasty side, slice ripe tomatoes in half and sprinkle with minced garlic, Italian seasoning and grated Parmesan cheese. Broil until tomatoes are tender, about 5 minutes...scrumptious!

Mom's GO-TO Recipes

Potluck Pizza Casserole

Sheila Plock
Leland, NC

I took this casserole to many Cub Scout banquets! A great take-along dish for a family potluck dinner.

1 c. shell pasta, uncooked
1 c. rotini pasta, uncooked
1 c. elbow macaroni, uncooked
1 lb. ground beef
3/4 c. onion, diced
3/4 c. green pepper, diced
1/2 lb. sliced turkey pepperoni

8-oz. jar sliced mushrooms, drained
24-oz. jar spaghetti sauce
8-oz. pkg. shredded mozzarella cheese
Garnish: sliced fresh basil

Cook pastas together according to package directions, just until tender; drain. Meanwhile, brown beef with onion and green pepper in a large skillet over medium heat; drain. Add pepperoni and mushrooms. Simmer over medium-low heat for 15 minutes, stirring occasionally. Add cooked macaroni and spaghetti sauce to skillet; heat through. Transfer to a lightly greased 3-quart casserole dish; sprinkle with cheese. Bake at 350 degrees for 15 minutes, or until bubbly and cheese melts. Garnish with basil. Makes 6 servings.

Make some wonderful memories! Join your neighbors, family & friends in a good old-fashioned outdoor potluck. Set up the picnic table, break out the cornhole board, make pitchers of icy lemonade, arrange lots of chairs in the shade and invite everyone to bring their favorite dishes. Such fun!

Classic Oven-Baked COMFORT FOODS

Mac & Frank Casserole

Shirley Howie
Foxboro, MA

This is one of my best kid-friendly recipes! It can even be made ahead and popped in the oven at suppertime.

1-1/2 c. elbow macaroni,
   uncooked
10-3/4 oz. can Cheddar
   cheese soup
10-3/4 oz. can tomato soup

1/2 c. water
1/4 c. onion, minced
2 t. mustard
6 frankfurters

Cook macaroni according to package directions; drain. Meanwhile, heat cheese soup in a large saucepan over medium heat, stirring until smooth. Blend in tomato soup. Add water, onion and mustard; stir together. Add cooked macaroni; toss to mix well. Transfer to a greased 2-quart casserole dish; arrange frankfurters over macaroni mixture. Bake, uncovered, at 400 degrees for 25 minutes, or until hot and bubbly. Makes 4 to 6 servings.

A casserole that's baked uncovered will have a crisper, more golden topping than one that's covered during baking. It's your choice!

Mom's GO-TO *Recipes*

Cheesy Chicken Hot Dish

Sandra Sullivan
Aurora, CO

So good and hearty! This dish can be put together in 15 minutes.
Pop it in the oven for 20 minutes and dinner is served.

4 boneless, skinless chicken
   breasts, cut into 1-inch cubes
1 c. sliced mushrooms
10-3/4 oz. can cream of celery
   or chicken soup
15-oz. can peas, drained

2 c. cooked white rice
10-3/4 oz. can cream of
   mushroom soup
8-oz. pkg. shredded mozzarella
   cheese

Spray a skillet with non-stick vegetable spray. Heat over medium-high heat for about one minute; add chicken. Cook until golden and cooked through, about 15 minutes. Spray a shallow 3-quart casserole dish; transfer chicken to dish. Top with mushrooms; spoon soup over mushrooms. Top with peas and rice; spoon mushroom soup over rice. Sprinkle with cheese. Bake, uncovered, at 350 degrees for 20 minutes, or until bubbly and cheese is melted. Makes 4 servings.

Stir up a loaf of beer bread for dinner. Combine 3 cups self-rising flour, a 12-ounce can of beer and 3 tablespoons sugar in a greased loaf pan. Bake at 350 degrees for 25 minutes. Drizzle the loaf with melted butter and serve warm.

Classic Oven-Baked
COMFORT FOODS

One-Dish Steak Meal

Sandy Coffey
Cincinnati, OH

*A recipe from 1948, handed down by my grandmother and mother
to myself, my girls and my granddaughters. Easy to put together
ahead of time. Add a veggie and hot rolls and you are done.*

2 c. potatoes, peeled and diced
1/2 c. long-cooking rice,
　uncooked
1 c. onion, diced
1 lb. beef round steak, cut
　into strips

2 green peppers, diced
14-1/2 oz. can diced tomatoes
salt and pepper to taste
1 c. water

In a greased 3-quart casserole dish, layer ingredients as listed. Add salt
and pepper to taste. Pour water over all. Cover and bake at 350 degrees
for 1-1/2 hours. Makes 4 servings.

One-Pot Pesto Chicken

Rosemary Lightbown
Wakefield, RI

*This is a family favorite. You can also add different veggies to this.
I have used carrots, green beans, asparagus...be creative!*

6 chicken thighs and/or
　drumsticks
1-1/2 lbs. new redskin potatoes
1 pt. cherry tomatoes

1/2 c. basil pesto sauce
2 T. water
2 t. olive oil

Arrange chicken pieces in a lightly greased roasting pan. Scatter
potatoes and tomatoes around chicken; set aside. In a cup, stir together
pesto, water and olive oil. Spoon some of pesto mixture onto each
chicken piece; spoon the rest into the pan around the vegetables. Cover
and bake at 425 degrees for 45 minutes. Uncover and bake another
10 minutes. Makes 6 servings.

Save leftover pesto by spooning it into an ice cube tray. Once frozen,
bag up the cubes in a freezer bag until they're needed.

Mom's GO-TO *Recipes*

3-Cheese Pasta Bake

Lisanne Miller
Wells, ME

A sprinkle of nutmeg makes this dish outstanding! Serve it as
a side dish or meatless main, or carry it with pride to a potluck.

8-oz. pkg. penne pasta,
   uncooked
2 T. butter
2 T. all-purpose flour
1-1/2 c. milk
1/2 c. half-and-half
1/2 c. shredded white Cheddar
   cheese

1/4 c. grated Parmesan cheese
1 c. shredded Gruyère cheese,
   divided
1 t. salt
1/4 t. pepper
1/8 t. nutmeg

Cook pasta according to package directions; drain. Meanwhile, melt
butter in a saucepan over medium heat. Whisk in flour; cook for
one minute, whisking constantly. Gradually whisk in milk and half-
and-half; cook, whisking constantly, until thickened, 3 to 5 minutes.
Stir in Cheddar cheese, Parmesan cheese, 1/2 cup Gruyère cheese and
seasonings until smooth. Add cheese mixture to cooked pasta; mix well
and transfer to a lightly greased 11"x7" baking pan. Top with remaining
Gruyère cheese. Bake, uncovered, at 350 degrees for 15 minutes, or
until bubbly and cheese is melted. Makes 4 servings.

A crisp green salad goes well with all kinds of casseroles. For a zippy
dressing, shake up 1/2 cup olive oil, 1/3 cup lemon juice and
a tablespoon of Dijon mustard in a small jar and chill. You can
even shake it up in an almost-empty jar of mustard.

Classic Oven-Baked
COMFORT FOODS

Creole Zucchini

Naomi Townsend
Osage Beach, MO

When your neighbors leave a sack of zucchini squash at your doorstep,
surprise your family with this delicious side dish for dinner.

2 stalks celery, chopped
1/2 c. onion, chopped
1 green pepper, chopped
1 T. butter
15-1/2 oz. can petite diced
    tomatoes

8-oz. can tomato sauce
1 to 2 zucchini, cubed or sliced
sugar, salt and pepper to taste
Optional: bread cubes, grated
    Parmesan cheese

In a skillet over medium heat, sauté celery, onion and green pepper in
butter until celery is translucent. Stir in tomatoes with juice, tomato
sauce and zucchini; season with sugar, salt and pepper. Transfer mixture
to a buttered one-quart casserole dish. Top with bread cubes and cheese,
if desired. Bake, uncovered, at 350 degrees for 15 to 20 minutes, until
bubbly and zucchini is tender. Makes 6 servings.

A crunchy crumb topping adds texture and flavor to casseroles.
Soft bread crumbs tossed with melted butter are the classic
crumb topping. Crushed tortilla chips, pretzels or savory
snack crackers are all tasty too.

Mom's GO-TO Recipes

Shrimp & Confetti Rice

Tina Wright
Atlanta, GA

My older kids love to help put together these festive foil packets for dinner. Pop them in the oven and before you know it, it's time for dinner! In the summertime, these can be grilled on a covered grill for about 6 to 8 minutes.

1 lb. uncooked medium shrimp,
   peeled and cleaned
1-1/2 c. instant rice, uncooked
1/2 c. carrot, peeled and
   shredded
1/4 c. green onions, sliced

3/4 c. hot water
1/3 c. teriyaki marinade
2 t. sesame oil
1/2 t. garlic powder
Optional: 2 T. sliced almonds

In a large bowl, combine all ingredients except almonds; toss to mix well. Spoon 1/4 of shrimp mixture into the center of an 18-inch length of non-stick aluminum foil. Bring up sides of foil. Double-fold the top and ends to seal packet, leaving room for heat circulation inside. Repeat to make 3 more packets. Place packets on a large baking sheet; bake at 450 degrees for 15 to 18 minutes. Open packets carefully; sprinkle with almonds, if desired. Makes 4 servings.

Keep frozen shrimp on hand for delicious meals anytime. Thaw it overnight in the fridge, or for a quicker way, place the frozen shrimp in a colander and run ice-cold water over it. Don't be tempted to thaw shrimp in the microwave, as it will get mushy.

Classic Oven-Baked
COMFORT FOODS

Squash Casserole

Vickie
Gooseberry Patch

There's something about a classic vegetable casserole that's impossible to resist. Even picky eaters go back for second helpings!

1-1/2 lbs. yellow squash,
   cut into 1/4-inch slices
1 lb. zucchini, cut into
   1/4-inch slices
1 sweet onion, chopped
2-1/2 t. salt, divided
1 c. carrots, peeled grated
10-3/4-oz. can cream of
   chicken soup

8-oz. container sour cream
8-oz. can water chestnuts,
   drained and chopped
8-oz. pkg. herb-flavored
   stuffing mix
1/2 c. butter, melted

Place squash and zucchini in a Dutch oven. Add chopped onion, 2 teaspoons salt and enough water to cover. Bring to a boil over medium-high heat and cook 5 minutes; drain well. Stir together carrot, next 3 ingredients and remaining salt in a large bowl; fold in squash mixture. Stir together stuffing mix and melted butter; spoon half of stuffing mixture into bottom of a lightly greased 13"x9" baking pan. Spoon squash mixture over stuffing mixture and top with remaining stuffing mixture. Bake at 350 degrees for 30 to 35 minutes or until bubbly and golden, covering with aluminum foil after 20 to 25 minutes to prevent excessive browning, if necessary. Let stand 10 minutes before serving. Serves 8.

Make a simple, satisfying side in a jiffy with a package of thin spaghetti. Toss cooked pasta with a little butter and grated Parmesan cheese, or try chopped fresh tomato and a drizzle of olive oil.

Mom's GO-TO *Recipes*

Twice-Baked Potato Casserole

Robin Hill
Rochester, NY

This is my favorite recipe whenever we're hosting a cookout or tailgate...everyone loves it, and I love that I can make it ahead and warm it up later. Just add some grilled burgers and brats and a big tossed salad for the best party meal ever.

5 lbs. russet potatoes
8-oz. pkg. cream cheese, room
   temperature
1/2 c. butter, room temperature
16-oz. container sour cream,
   room temperature
8-oz. pkg. shredded sharp
   Cheddar cheese, divided

2 cloves garlic, minced
1-1/2 t. salt
1/2 t. pepper
6 slices thick-cut bacon, crisply
   cooked and crumbled
1/4 c. green onions, chopped

Pierce potatoes with a fork; place on oven racks. Bake at 350 degrees for 60 to 75 minutes, until very tender. Peel potatoes; cube them into a large bowl. Add cream cheese, butter, sour cream and one cup Cheddar cheese. Stir until well combined; stir in garlic, salt and pepper. Transfer potato mixture to a greased 13"x9" baking pan. Bake, uncovered, at 350 degrees for 30 to 35 minutes, until heated through. Sprinkle with remaining cheese; bake another 5 minutes, or until cheese melts. Garnish with crumbled bacon and green onions. Serves 10 to 12.

Cooking for just a few? Use two 8"x8" baking pans instead of one 13"x9". Enjoy one dish for dinner tonight, and freeze the other for a future no-fuss meal!

Classic Oven-Baked
COMFORT FOODS

Greek Chicken & Potatoes

Sharon Demers
Bruce Crossing, MI

A gourmet dinner-in-one without much effort...especially delicious
with Yukon Gold potatoes! Just add a zesty tossed salad
and dinner is served.

1-1/3 lbs. potatoes, peeled
    and sliced
1/2 c. sliced Kalamata olives,
    drained
2 cloves garlic, minced
1 t. dried oregano

2 t. salt
1 t. pepper
4 boneless, skinless chicken
    breasts
Garnish: diced tomatoes,
    crumbled feta cheese

In a bowl, combine potatoes, olives, garlic and seasonings; mix well.
Divide mixture evenly among 4 squares of heavy-duty aluminum foil.
Top each with one chicken breast. Fold over top edges, then fold in
sides, creating packets. Place on baking sheets. Bake at 450 degrees for
35 to 40 minutes. To serve, carefully open tops of packets; check for
doneness of chicken. Serve directly from packets, or transfer to plates;
garnish with tomatoes and cheese. Serves 4.

Make a chopped salad in seconds...no cutting board needed!
Add all the salad fixings except dressing to a big bowl, then
roll a pizza cutter back & forth over them. Drizzle with
dressing and enjoy your salad.

King Ranch Chicken

Wendy Reaume
Ontario, Canada

This dish has a bit of a Tex-Mex flair mixed with a chicken & noodles kind of heartiness. When I was in college, they used to serve a similar dish in the dining room, and everyone always lined up quickly for it. After I graduated, I went on a mission to recreate it. As a busy mom, I love it because assembly is quick...and it's so easy to make ahead of time to pop in the freezer.

1 onion, chopped
2 t. olive oil
10-3/4 oz. can cream of
   chicken soup
10-3/4 oz. cream of
   mushroom soup
14-1/2 oz. can fire-roasted or
   regular diced tomatoes
4-oz. can chopped green chiles

1/2 t. sea salt
1/2 t. pepper
10-oz. pkg. tortilla chips, crushed
2-1/2 lb. deli rotisserie chicken,
   shredded, bones and skin
   discarded
3 to 4 c. shredded Cheddar
   cheese, divided

In a skillet over medium heat, sauté onion in olive oil until golden. Add soups, tomatoes with juice and chiles, salt and pepper; mix well. Spread crushed tortilla chips in a greased 13"x9" baking pan. Spoon half of soup mixture over chips. Top with all of the chicken and half of cheese. Spoon remaining soup mixture over top. Cover tightly with aluminum foil. Bake at 400 degrees for 20 minutes. Remove foil and top with remaining cheese. Bake, uncovered, another 20 minutes, until cheese is bubbly and starts to brown. Serves 8.

Serve up icy lemonade in frosted-rim glasses. Chill tumblers in the fridge. At serving time, moisten rims with lemon juice or water and dip into a dish of sparkling sugar.

Slow-Cooker
FAMILY
FAVORITES

Mom's GO-TO *Recipes*

Ham & Scalloped Potatoes

LaShelle Brown
Mulvane, KS

This is one of my favorite, hearty meals for busy days.

1/2 t. cream of tartar
1 c. cold water
8 potatoes, peeled and thinly
   sliced
2 16-oz. cooked ham steaks,
   1/2-inch thick, cubed and
   divided

1 onion, chopped and divided
salt and pepper to taste
1 c. shredded Cheddar cheese,
   divided
10-3/4 oz. can cream of celery
   soup, divided
paprika to taste

In a large bowl, dissolve cream of tartar in cold water. Add potato slices;
toss to coat and drain. In a 5-quart slow cooker, layer half each of the
ham, potatoes and onion; season with salt and pepper and sprinkle with
half of the cheese. Repeat layering. Spoon soup over top; sprinkle with
paprika. Cover and cook on low setting for 8 hours, or until bubbly and
potatoes are tender. Makes 8 servings.

Slow cookers are super year 'round...no matter what the occasion!
Fill up the slow cooker, then pack up the family and head out to
a local ball game, festival or nature walk. When you come home,
a delicious meal will be waiting for you.

Slow-Cooker
FAMILY FAVORITES

Chicken Pot Pie

Mallory Lanning
Minden, LA

Down-home flavor, yet oh-so easy! My husband and I both enjoy flaky biscuits crumbled into our bowls, while my kids like grilled cheese on the side. It's a quick meal to put together.

2 10-3/4 oz. cans cream of
   chicken soup
2 to 2-1/2 c. milk
1-oz. pkg chicken gravy mix
1/4 t. dried parsley
1/8 t. garlic powder
1/8 t. dried basil

1/4 t. salt
1/8 t. pepper
1 lb. boneless, skinless chicken
   breasts, cubed
8-oz. pkg. frozen mixed
   vegetables

In a bowl, whisk together soup, milk, gravy mix and seasonings. Pour into a greased 5-quart slow cooker; add chicken and vegetables. Cover and cook on low for 7 to 8 hours, or on high setting for 3-1/2 to 4 hours. Makes 6 servings.

Slice or dice uncooked meat in a jiffy! Just pop it in the freezer
for 10 to 15 minutes first, until it's slightly frozen.

Mom's GO-TO *Recipes*

Pork Chops with Gravy

Brandie Skibinski
Salem, VA

This is definitely my go-to meal for busy weeknights. I almost always have everything I need on hand. I just pop it all in my slow cooker... by the end of the day, the meal is ready for my family!

4 thick bone-in pork chops
10-3/4 oz. can cream of chicken
   or mushroom soup
1-1/2 c. chicken broth

1-oz. pkg. onion soup mix
1-oz. pkg. pork gravy mix
mashed potatoes

Arrange pork chops in a 4-quart slow cooker. In a bowl, mix remaining ingredients except potatoes; spoon over pork chops. Cover and cook on low setting for 6 to 8 hours. Serve with mashed potatoes, topped with gravy from slow cooker. Serves 4.

Ranch Pork Chops

Pamela Myers
Auburn, IN

This is a great meal...it's my tried & true recipe whenever I want to make pork chops for dinner. After slow cooking all day, the pork chops are fall-apart tender. It also makes a delicious gravy that I serve over mashed potatoes.

4 to 6 boneless pork chops
1-oz. pkg. ranch salad dressing
   mix

10-3/4 oz. can cream of
   chicken soup

Place pork chops in a 4-quart slow cooker; sprinkle with dressing mix. Spread soup over pork chops. Cover and cook on low setting for 6 to 8 hours. Makes 4 to 6 servings.

To make clean-up a breeze, lightly spray the inside of a slow cooker with non-stick vegetable spray before adding recipe ingredients. What a time-saver!

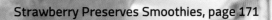

Strawberry Preserves Smoothies, page 171

Cranberry Upside-Down Muffins, page 23

Peachy Baked Oatmeal, page 20

Sunrise Skillet, page 10

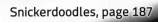
Snickerdoodles, page 187

Ranch Ham & Tortilla Pinwheels, page 163

3-Cheese Pasta Bake, page 116

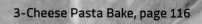

Calico Corn Salsa, page 157

Avocado-Feta Dip, page 153

Tomato-Basil Soup, page 33

Grilled Reuben Sandwich, page 42

Confetti Coleslaw, page 51

Super-Simple Salmon
Patties, page 79

Frozen Peanut Butter
Pie, page 207

Country-Style Creamed Corn, page 133

One-Pot Pork Chop Dinner, page 58

Fruit & Nut Chicken Salad, page 38

Gobblin' Good Turkey Burgers, page 66

Diana's Carrot Sheet Cake, page 204

Plenty o' Veggies Beef Stew, page 143

Peanut Butter & Jelly Bars, page 199

Potluck Pizza Casserole, page 112

Squash Casserole, page 119

Mom's Best Fruit Smoothies, page 24

Slow-Cooker
FAMILY FAVORITES

Texas Potatoes

*Tina Schwab
South Attleboro, MA*

*This is my tried & true potluck dish. I always keep a few
copies of the recipe on hand to hand out.*

10-3/4 oz. can cream of
   mushroom soup
1-1/2 c. sour cream
16-oz. pkg. shredded
   Cheddar cheese

1/2 c. cream cheese, softened
30-oz. pkg. frozen diced
   hashbrowns
3/4 c. onion, chopped

In a large bowl, combine soup, sour cream and cheeses; mix thoroughly.
Add potatoes and onion; mix gently. Transfer mixture to a lightly
greased 6-quart slow cooker. Cover and cook on low setting for 8 to
10 hours, until hot and bubbly. Makes 10 to 12 servings.

Try your favorite slow-cooker meat recipe in your electric pressure
cooker! If the dish cooks on low for 8 hours or on high for 4 hours,
it will cook in about 25 to 30 minutes in the pressure cooker.
Be sure to set it to "sealing" (not "venting") and make sure
there's a cup of liquid in the recipe.

Mom's GO-TO *Recipes*

Nacho Chicken Spaghetti

Nancy Kailihiwa
Wheatland, CA

Feeding a bunch of teenage boys has to be easy and fast! This recipe
is a real crowd-pleaser. It would be great for potlucks too...
just double the recipe in a larger slow cooker.

2 to 3 boneless, skinless chicken
    breasts, diced
14-oz. can diced tomatoes with
    green chiles
16-oz. pkg. spaghetti, uncooked
1/2 c. sour cream

10-3/4 oz. can cream of chicken
    soup
3 c. shredded mild Cheddar Jack
    cheese
Optional: several drops hot
    pepper sauce

In a 4-quart slow cooker, combine chicken and tomatoes with juice.
Cover and cook on low setting for 4 hours. Cook spaghetti according to
package directions; drain and add to slow cooker. Stir in sour cream and
soup. Top with cheese; stir again. Cover and cook on low setting for
an additional 2 hours. Stir just before serving; add hot sauce to taste,
if desired. Serves 6 to 8.

When you put away groceries, be sure to label any ingredients
that are intended for dinner...that way, Wednesday's supper won't
turn into Tuesday's after-school snack! Set aside cubed cheese,
veggies and fruit labeled "OK for snacking" to tame appetites.

Slow-Cooker
FAMILY FAVORITES

Homestyle Mac & Cheese

JoAnn Barnes
Alden, NY

When my boys were small, I would cook this meal whenever we were raking leaves in our country yard. When we came back into the house afterwards, the house always smelled divine and my sons devoured the mac & cheese with delight. I like to serve it with a green salad and some crusty bread & butter.

8-oz. pkg. elbow macaroni,
    uncooked
12-oz. can evaporated milk
1-1/2 c. whole milk
2 eggs, beaten
1/4 c. butter, melted

1 t. salt
1/8 t. pepper
5 c. shredded sharp Cheddar
    cheese, divided
1/8 t. paprika

Cook macaroni according to package directions. Drain; transfer to a 4-quart slow cooker sprayed with non-stick vegetable spray. Add milks, eggs, butter, salt, pepper and all except 1/2 cup of shredded cheese. Mix well; sprinkle with reserved cheese and paprika. Cover and cook on low setting for 3 hours and 15 minutes. Turn off the slow cooker. Stir, then cover with Crunchy Topping. Makes 8 to 10 servings.

Crunchy Topping:

1 T. butter

3 c. corn flake cereal, crushed

Melt butter in a skillet over medium heat. Add cereal and cook until golden, stirring constantly.

For the best results from your slow cooker, make sure
it's filled from 1/2 to 2/3 full.

Mom's GO-TO Recipes

El Paso Soup

Carolyn Britton
Millry, AL

Quick & easy, this recipe is a great hit with children and adults.
Perfect for a ballgame treat!

2 lbs. ground turkey
3/4 c. onion, chopped
14-1/2 oz. can diced tomatoes
10-oz. can diced tomatoes
   with green chiles
2 11-oz. cans white
   shoepeg corn
15-1/2 oz. can red kidney beans

15-1/2 oz. can pinto beans
15-1/2 oz. can black beans
2 1-1/4 oz. pkgs. taco seasoning
   mix
2 1-oz. pkgs. ranch salad
   dressing mix
Garnish: shredded Cheddar
   cheese, tortilla chips

Brown turkey and onion in a skillet over medium heat; drain. Combine turkey mixture, tomatoes with juice and remaining ingredients except garnish in a 6-quart slow cooker. Cover and cook on low setting for 2 to 3 hours. If mixture is too thick, stir in a little extra broth or water. Serve topped with shredded cheese and tortilla chips. Serves 12 to 15.

Slow cookers come in so many sizes...what to choose?
The 4-quart size is handy for recipes that will feed 4 people, while
5-1/2 to 6 quarts is just right for larger families and potlucks.
Just have room for one? Choose an oval slow cooker...
whole chickens and pot roasts will fit perfectly.

Slow-Cooker
FAMILY FAVORITES

Easy Mexican Chicken

Jana Pedowitz
Marina Del Rey, CA

This is the best recipe for quick & easy! I love this
for a quick night-in meal.

4 boneless, skinless chicken
    breasts
16-oz. jar favorite salsa
15-1/2 oz. can black beans

1-1/4 oz. pkg. taco
    seasoning mix
warm tortillas or tortilla chips

Layer all ingredients except tortillas or tortilla chips in a 5-quart slow cooker. Stir to mix in seasoning. Cover and cook on low setting for 8 hours. Shred chicken with 2 forks; stir back into mixture in slow cooker. Serve with tortillas or tortilla chips. Makes 6 servings.

When toting slow-cooker dishes to a potluck, tie a colorful
bandanna onto the lid and slip a wooden spoon inside
the knot. A clever way to wrap it all up!

Mom's GO-TO *Recipes*

Parmesan Chicken & Rice

Linda Belon
Wintersville, OH

*This is a delicious slow-cooker version of our old favorite,
no-peek chicken. Chicken and rice all in one...just add
a salad and dinner is served.*

4 boneless, skinless chicken
   breasts
salt and pepper to taste
4 T. butter, sliced
10-3/4 oz. can cream of
   mushroom soup

1-1/2 c. milk
1 c. water
1-1/2 oz. pkg. onion soup mix
1 c. long-cooking rice, uncooked
1/2 c. grated Parmesan cheese

Season chicken with salt and pepper; arrange in a greased 5-quart slow
cooker. Top each piece of chicken with one tablespoon butter; set aside.
In a bowl, mix together remaining ingredients except Parmesan cheese;
spoon over chicken. Sprinkle with cheese. Cover and cook on low
setting for 8 to 10 hours, or on high setting for 4 to 6 hours. Serves 4.

Make family mealtimes special! Even when you don't have guests
coming, pull out the good china, set a vase of flowers on the table
and light some candles. It's a terrific time to encourage children's
good table manners...and make memories together too.

Slow-Cooker FAMILY FAVORITES

Farmstyle Green Beans

Vickie
Gooseberry Patch

*Slow-simmered fresh green beans are our treat after
we've shopped at the farmers' market.*

1 yellow onion, diced
2 cloves garlic, minced
2 T. olive oil
14-oz. can chicken broth

2 lbs. fresh green beans,
   snapped
1/2 t. garlic salt
salt and pepper to taste

In a skillet over medium heat, sauté onion and garlic in oil for 4 to
5 minutes, until tender. Transfer mixture to a 5-quart slow cooker; add
remaining ingredients. Cover and cook on low setting for 3-1/2 to
4 hours, to desired tenderness. Serves 8.

Country-Style Creamed Corn

Judy Taylor
Butler, MO

*Tastes like homegrown corn! This has become a family tradition.
We have a large family, and this is something everyone enjoys.*

2 16-oz. pkgs. frozen corn
8-oz. pkg. cream cheese, cubed
3/4 c. butter, cubed
2 T. sugar

3 T. water
1/2 t. salt
Optional: 2 T. grated Parmesan
   cheese, 1 t. dried basil

Add frozen corn to a 5-quart slow cooker; add remaining ingredients
and mix gently. Cover and cook on high setting for 45 minutes. Stir
with a wooden spoon. Reduce slow cooker setting to low; cook for
3-1/2 hours, stirring occasionally. Stir in cheese and basil, if using, just
before serving. Makes 8 to 10 servings.

Mom's GO-TO Recipes

One-Pot Beef & Bean Dinner

Sereena Shailer
Sunland, CA

Delicious served with mashed potatoes or a big pan of cornbread.

1 lb. ground beef
1/2 lb. bacon
1 c. onion, chopped
1 c. catsup
1/4 c. brown sugar, packed
3 T. white vinegar
1 t. smoke-flavored cooking
   sauce
1 t. salt

1/8 t. pepper
16-oz. can vegetarian baked
   beans
15-oz. can pork & beans
15-1/2 oz. can kidney beans,
   drained
15-1/2 oz. can black beans,
   drained

Brown beef in a skillet over medium; drain and set aside. In the same skillet, cook bacon with onion until crisp; drain. In a 5-quart slow cooker, mix together catsup, brown sugar, vinegar, sauce, salt and pepper. Add beef, bacon mixture and beans; stir well. Cover and cook on low setting for 4 to 5 hours. Makes 8 servings.

Mashed potatoes are the perfect side dish for so many comfort food favorites! Try a delicious secret...substitute equal parts chicken broth and cream for the milk in any favorite recipe.

Slow-Cooker
FAMILY FAVORITES

Everything-But-the-Kitchen-Sink Mexican Chicken

Emily Salsky
Mesa, AZ

This is my go-to chicken recipe for all kinds of Mexican meals! Use it to fill enchiladas, quesadillas or chalupas, or serve it over rice with cheese. It's easy, nutritious and best of all, delicious.

2 to 3 boneless, skinless
　chicken breasts
1 green pepper, chopped
1 red pepper, chopped
1 onion, chopped
16-oz. jar favorite salsa
10-oz. pkg. frozen corn

10-oz. can diced tomatoes with
　green chiles
Optional: 15-1/2 oz. can black
　or pinto beans
1-oz. pkg. taco seasoning mix
ground cumin, salt and pepper
　to taste

Combine all ingredients in a 5-quart slow cooker; stir to mix well. Cover and cook on low setting for 8 hours. Shred chicken with a fork; stir back into mixture in slow cooker. Serve as desired. Makes 6 servings.

Don't hesitate to stock up on frozen vegetables! Time-saving blends and mixes speed things up when it's time to make dinner. Flash-frozen soon after being harvested, they're flavorful, colorful and good for you.

Mom's GO-TO *Recipes*

Hearty Steak Soup

Connie Armstrong
Gardner, KS

*My family starts looking forward to this hearty, veggie-filled
soup as soon as the weather begins to turn cool. It tastes just
as good the next day, too!*

1 lb. lean ground beef
3/4 c. onion, chopped
1 c. potatoes, peeled and cubed
1 c. carrots, peeled and sliced
16-oz. pkg. frozen mixed
    vegetables

2 10-3/4 oz. cans cream of
    celery soup
2 c. vegetable cocktail juice
1 t. salt

In a Dutch oven over medium heat, cook beef with onion until browned;
drain. Add remaining ingredients; reduce heat to medium-low and
simmer for 45 minutes. Transfer soup to a slow cooker. Cover and
cook on low setting for 6 to 8 hours. Serves 6.

Laughter really is the best medicine! Studies show all kinds of health
benefits come from time spent laughing...it can even burn extra
calories. So be sure to share funny stories and even the kids'
latest jokes everyday over dinner.

Slow-Cooker
FAMILY FAVORITES

Hearty Tomato-Beef Stew

Bethi Hendrickson
Danville, PA

*This recipe is a true comfort dish! Serve with warm bread
and you have a winner.*

1-1/2 lbs. stew beef cubes
3 stalks celery, thinly sliced
6 carrots, peeled and thinly sliced

7 to 8 potatoes, peeled and diced
2 10-3/4 oz. cans tomato soup
2 T. celery seed

In a lightly greased 6-quart slow cooker, combine beef and vegetables.
Spoon soup over top; sprinkle with celery seed and mix thoroughly.
Cover and cook on low setting for 8 to 9 hours, or on high setting for
4 to 5 hours. Serves 8.

Biscuit toppers make a hearty meal of a bowl of stew. Flatten jumbo
refrigerated biscuits and arrange on an ungreased baking sheet.
Pierce several times with a fork and bake as package directs. Place
each topper on a bowl of hot stew and serve.

Mom's GO-TO Recipes

Best-Ever Chili Dogs

Marlene Swisher
Reading, KS

This recipe is great to use while you're at a school activity or some other event. The ingredients cook while you're away.

8 hot dogs
2 15-oz. cans chili without
   beans
10-3/4 oz. can Cheddar
   cheese soup

4-oz. can chopped green chiles
8 hot dog buns, split
3/4 c. onion, chopped
1 to 2 c. corn chips, crushed
1 c. shredded Cheddar cheese

Place hot dogs in a 4-quart slow cooker; set aside. In a bowl, combine chili, soup and chiles; spoon over hot dogs. Cover and cook on low setting for 4 to 5 hours. Serve hot dogs in buns, topped with chili mixture, onion, corn chips and cheese. Serves 8 to 10.

Ballpark Hot Dogs

Diana Krol
Hutchinson, KS

I don't eat hot dogs myself, but I've fixed thousands this way for our baseball concession stand. The hot dogs cook slowly in their own juices, and the whole house smells good. I also like to cook Polish sausage this way.

8 to 16 hot dogs
8 to 16 hot dog buns, split

Garnish: favorite hot dog
   condiments

Place hot dogs in a 4-quart slow cooker; do not add any liquid. Cover and cook on high setting for 2 hours, or on low setting for up to 5 hours. Serve hot dogs right from the slow cooker with your favorite buns and condiments. Makes 8 to 16 servings.

Slow-Cooker
FAMILY FAVORITES

Sweet & Spicy Sloppy Joes

Tina Hanks
Wilmington, OH

This was always a family favorite for my husband and children, especially around football season. We used to gather around the TV and enjoy the game while eating these Sloppy Joes.

2 lbs. ground beef
3/4 c. onion, chopped
3/4 c. green pepper, chopped
3/4 c. fresh or canned jalapeños,
    chopped and seeds removed
1-1/2 c. catsup

6-oz. can tomato paste
1/2 c. brown sugar, packed
1/4 c. Worcestershire sauce
1 T. mustard
1/2 t. full-flavor molasses
12 hamburger buns, split

In a skillet over medium heat, cook beef with onion until no longer pink; drain. Transfer to a 5-quart slow cooker; stir in remaining ingredients except buns. Cover and cook on low setting for 2 to 4 hours, until thickened and vegetables are soft. To serve, spoon onto buns. Makes 12 servings.

Pick up a stack of retro-style plastic burger baskets. Lined with crisp paper napkins, they're still such fun for serving hot dogs, burgers and fries.

Mom's GO-TO *Recipes*

Applesauce BBQ Pulled Pork

Kristin Pittis
Dennison, OH

Just a little sweet and really good! Just add some crunchy coleslaw and potato chips for an easy casual meal.

1 onion, coarsely chopped
2 to 3-lb. pork roast
1/2 t. salt
1/4 t. pepper

1/2 c. unsweetened applesauce, divided
1/2 c. barbecue sauce
8 hamburger buns, split

Spread onion in a greased 4-quart slow cooker. Place roast on top; season with salt and pepper. Spread 1/4 cup applesauce over roast. Cover and cook on low setting for 8 hours. Remove roast and onion to a platter; shred roast. Drain slow cooker, reserving 2 tablespoons cooking liquid. Return shredded pork and onions to slow cooker along with reserved liquid, remaining applesauce and barbecue sauce. Cover and cook on low setting for 30 minutes, or until heated through. Serve on buns. Makes 8 servings.

Just for fun, spear cherry tomatoes, cheese cubes or
tiny gherkin pickles with a toothpick and use
to fasten party sandwiches.

Slow-Cooker
FAMILY FAVORITES

Cream Cheese Chicken

Leona Krivda
Belle Vernon, PA

This is so good you can't stay out of it! It is so easy and you can either serve it on buns, or just on a plate as I do. Great to make on a day you are short on time.

4 boneless, skinless chicken
  breasts
1-oz. pkg. ranch salad dressing
  mix
8-oz. pkg. cream cheese, room
  temperature, cubed
1/4 c. butter, sliced

salt, pepper, garlic powder and
  turmeric to taste
1/2 c. bacon, crisply cooked and
  crumbled
1/2 c. shredded Cheddar cheese
Optional: 6 to 8 buns, split;
  barbecue sauce

Layer chicken breasts in a 4-quart slow cooker coated with non-stick spray. Sprinkle with dressing mix; top with cream cheese and butter. Cover and cook on high setting for 4 to 5 hours, until chicken is tender. Remove chicken to a bowl. Shred with a fork and season lightly with salt; set aside. Whisk cooking liquid in slow cooker to break up any pieces of cream cheese; add seasonings as desired. Return shredded chicken to slow cooker; stir to coat well. Set slow cooker to low or warm. At serving time, add bacon and Cheddar cheese and stir again. If desired, spoon into buns; top with barbecue sauce. Serves 6 to 8.

When you look at your life, the greatest happinesses
are family happinesses.

– Dr. Joyce Brothers

Mom's GO-TO Recipes

Baked Potato Soup

Ann Davis
Brookville, IN

*I love slow-cooker meals! This is always a yummy dinner, even on
busy days. Easy too...you don't even peel the potatoes.*

5 lbs. baking potatoes, cubed
3/4 c. yellow onion, diced
8 c. chicken broth
5 t. garlic, minced
2 to 3 t. salt

2 8-oz. pkgs. cream cheese,
  softened
Garnish: crumbled bacon,
  shredded Cheddar cheese

In a 6-quart slow cooker, combine potatoes, onion, broth, garlic and
salt. Cover and cook on high setting for 6 hours, or until potatoes are
very tender. Stir cream cheese into soup until melted. Top servings with
crumbled bacon and shredded cheese. Makes 8 to 10 servings.

For thick, creamy vegetable soup, use a hand-held immersion
blender to purée some of the cooked veggies right in
the slow cooker.

Slow-Cooker
FAMILY FAVORITES

Plenty o' Veggies Beef Stew

Paula Marchesi
Lenhartsville, PA

This is a hearty yet super-easy stew that your family is sure to like. It goes together in a jiffy...I open all the cans while the beef is browning. To change it up just a little, I'll use browned ground beef instead of stew beef, or add a handful of alphabet macaroni, just for fun!

8 slices bacon, diced
3 lbs. stew beef, cubed
6 carrots, peeled and thickly
    sliced
6 tomatoes, peeled and cut into
    wedges
4 potatoes, peeled and cubed
3 c. butternut squash, peeled
    and cubed

1/2 c. frozen lima beans
1/2 c. corn
2 cloves garlic, minced
2 t. dried thyme
2 14-1/2 oz. cans beef broth
6 c. cabbage, chopped
1/2 t. celery salt
1/2 t. pepper

In a large skillet over medium heat, cook bacon until crisp. Remove bacon to paper towels with a slotted spoon and refrigerate; reserve pan drippings. Brown beef in batches in reserved drippings; drain. In a 6-quart slow cooker, combine carrots, tomatoes, potatoes, squash, beans, corn, garlic and thyme. Top with beef. Pour broth into slow cooker. Cover and cook on low setting for 8 hours. Stir in cabbage and seasonings. Cover; increase to high setting and cook for 30 to 35 minutes, until cabbage is tender. Sprinkle servings with bacon. Makes 10 to 12 servings.

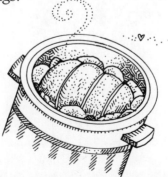

Less-tender cuts of beef like chuck roast and round steak
become fork-tender and delicious after slow-cooking
all day...they're budget-friendly too.

Mom's GO-TO Recipes

Spicy Sausage Chili

Sena Horn
Payson, UT

This is delicious just as it's written...very spicy and flavorful. It's extra special garnished with shredded cheese, sour cream, sliced avocados, chopped green onions, a squeeze of fresh lime and taco chips! It's a favorite at at family gatherings and potlucks.

1 lb. ground beef	3 to 4 T. chili powder
1 lb. mild Italian ground	1-1/2 t. ground cumin
pork sausage	1-1/2 t. garlic powder
46-oz. can tomato juice	1/2 t. dried oregano
29-oz. can tomato sauce	1 t. salt
15-1/2 oz. can kidney beans	1/2 t. pepper
3/4 c. onion, chopped	1/2 t. sugar
1 green pepper, diced	Optional: 1/8 t. cayenne pepper
1/2 c. celery, diced	juice of 1 lime

In a large skillet over medium heat, brown beef and sausage together; drain. Transfer beef mixture to a 6-quart slow cooker. Add remaining ingredients and stir together well. Cover and cook on low setting for 3 to 4 hours. Makes 8 to 10 servings.

A simple bouquet that's perfect for a casual supper! Pick up a bunch of dewy-fresh cut flowers at the local market and tuck them into a canning jar.

Slow-Cooker FAMILY FAVORITES

Pasta e Fagioli

Jeanne Koebel
Adirondack, NY

A hearty soup for cold or chilly days! Pair with a tossed salad
and warm bread for a great meal anytime.

1 lb. ground beef or turkey
1/2 c. onion, chopped
2 stalks celery, chopped
2 carrots, peeled and chopped
2 t. oil
32-oz. container unsalted
    vegetable or beef broth
2 14-1/2 oz. cans Italian-style
    stewed tomatoes
2 8-oz. cans tomato sauce

15-1/2 oz. can dark red kidney
    beans, drained
15-1/2 oz. can Great Northern
    beans, drained
1 t. Italian seasoning
1 t. dried basil
3/4 t. garlic powder
16-oz. pkg. ditalini pasta,
    uncooked

Brown beef or turkey in a skillet over medium heat. Drain; add to a
6-quart slow cooker and set aside. In the same skillet, sauté onion,
celery and carrots in oil; add to slow cooker. Add remaining ingredients
except pasta; stir well. Cover and cook on low setting for 8 to 10 hours.
Shortly before serving, separately cook desired amount of pasta; add to
servings of soup. Makes 8 servings.

Pop some delicious Parmesan bread in the oven. Blend 1/4 cup
butter, 2 tablespoons grated Parmesan cheese, 2 teaspoons minced
garlic and 1/4 teaspoon Italian seasoning. Spread it over a
halved loaf of French bread and broil until golden.

Mom's GO-TO Recipes

Mindy's Barbecue Pork Roast

Beth Bundy
Long Prairie, MN

A great recipe from my friend Mindy. Any leftovers make delicious sandwiches!

1 onion, thinly sliced
1 T. all-purpose flour
2 to 3-lb. pork shoulder roast
18-oz. bottle barbecue sauce,
    divided

1 T. chili powder
1 t. ground cumin

Spread onion slices in a 5-quart slow cooker. Sprinkle flour over onion; add roast to slow cooker and set aside. Combine one cup barbecue sauce and seasonings in a bowl; mix well and spoon over roast. Cover and cook on low setting for 10 to 12 hours, until roast is very tender. Remove roast to a platter; slice or shred. Drizzle with remaining barbecue sauce. Makes 4 to 6 servings.

Slow-cook a pot of creamy beans to serve with pork dishes. Rinse and drain 1/2 pound dried navy beans. Add them to a slow cooker and stir in a chopped onion, a tablespoon of bacon drippings or butter and 5 cups boiling water. Cover and cook on high for 4 hours, stirring occasionally. Don't add salt until the beans are tender. So easy!

Slow-Cooker
FAMILY FAVORITES

Easy Cheesy Potatoes

Bethi Hendrickson
Danville, PA

These creamy, cheesy potatoes are an added bonus
to any meal. Oh-so good!

5 to 7 Yukon Gold potatoes,
   thinly sliced
2 10-3/4 oz. cans Cheddar
   cheese soup

1 c. milk
8-oz. pkg. shredded Cheddar
   cheese, divided

Add sliced potatoes to a large bowl; set aside. In a saucepan, combine soup and milk. Cook and stir over medium heat until creamy and warmed through. Pour soup mixture over potatoes and mix thoroughly. In a greased 6-quart slow cooker, add a layer of potato mixture, then a light layer of shredded cheese. Continue, making several layers and ending with cheese on top. Cover and cook on low setting for 7 to 8 hours, or on high setting for 5 to 6 hours. Serves 8 to 10.

To remove cooked-on drips inside a slow-cooker base, remove the crock liner and set it aside. Fill a mug with ammonia and carefully set it in the slow cooker. Cover and let stand all night. In the morning, discard the cup of ammonia...any stains will wipe away easily. If any gunk remains, scrub it off with a paste of hydrogen peroxide and baking soda.

Mom's GO-TO *Recipes*

Cozy Cabbage Casserole

Marsha Baker
Pioneer, OH

This is such a delicious, filling dish, especially in cooler weather. Sometimes I will spice it up by substituting salsa for half of the spaghetti sauce. Serve over cooked rice, if you like...it's mighty good just as it is!

1 lb. ground beef
1/2 head cabbage, chopped
   and divided
3/4 c. onion, chopped and
   divided

18-oz. jar spaghetti sauce,
   divided
garlic powder, salt and pepper
   to taste
1 c. water

Brown beef in a skillet over medium heat; drain and set aside. In a 5-quart slow cooker, layer half each of cabbage, onion, beef and spaghetti sauce. Repeat layering, adding seasonings as desired. Pour water into slow cooker around the sides. Cover and cook on low setting for 6 to 7 hours, or on high setting for 3 to 4 hours. Makes 6 servings.

Take the kids along when you visit a farmers' market. Let each child choose a vegetable and let them help prepare it. Even picky eaters will want to taste-test their very own veggies!

Slow-Cooker
FAMILY FAVORITES

Chicken & Stars Soup

Claudia Keller
Carrollton, GA

This recipe is my secret weapon whenever one of the kids comes down with sniffles. Can't beat a big crock full of made-from-scratch chicken soup for chasing the chills!

4 to 6 chicken thighs
4 carrots, peeled and sliced
4 stalks celery, sliced
1 onion, peeled and halved
2 cloves garlic, minced
2 bay leaves
1 t. salt
1/4 t. pepper
6 c. water
2 cubes chicken bouillon
1/2 c. small star pasta, uncooked
Optional: 1/4 c. fresh parsley,
    chopped

Remove skins from chicken thighs, if desired. Arrange chicken in a 6-quart slow cooker. Add vegetables, garlic, bay leaves, salt and pepper. Add water and bouillon cubes; stir. Cover and cook on low setting for 7 to 8 hours, or on high setting for 4 to 5 hours, until chicken is cooked through. About 20 minutes before serving, transfer chicken to a bowl; discard onion and bay leaves. Turn slow cooker to low setting, if needed. Stir in pasta; cover and cook until tender, 15 to 18 minutes. Shred chicken; stir into soup along with parsley, if desired. Makes 6 servings.

Adapt a family favorite soup, stew or chili to make in a slow cooker.
A recipe that simmers for 2 hours on the stovetop can usually
cook all day on the low setting without overcooking.

Mom's GO-TO *Recipes*

Easy-Peasy Dump Cake

LaDeana Cooper
Batavia, OH

*If you are looking for a surprisingly easy dessert, this is your
go-to recipe! I use it all year 'round...so delicious. There are
lots of different ways to make it, too, and they're all easy!*

21-oz. can fruit pie filling	1/2 c. butter, melted
18-1/4 oz. yellow cake mix	Garnish: ice cream

Spoon pie filling into a slow cooker; set aside. In a bowl, combine dry
cake mix and melted butter; mix until crumbly. Sprinkle cake mix over
pie filling; do not stir. Cover and cook on low setting for one to 2 hours.
To serve, spoon out portions and top with a scoop of ice cream. Makes
4 to 6 servings.

Variations:

Instead of fruit pie filling, use:

• one to 2 15-oz. cans sliced peaches, drained and 1/2 cup juice
reserved; add reserved juice along with peaches

• 2 to 3 c. fresh berries, sprinkled with 1/2 cup sugar and allowed to
"weep" until juicy

• 20-oz. pkg. frozen berries, thawed and one cup juice reserved; add
reserved juice along with berries

Garnish desserts with a strawberry fan...so pretty, yet so simple.
Starting at the tip, cut a strawberry into thin slices almost to
the stem. Carefully spread slices to form a fan.

Tasty Treats
ANYTIME

Mom's **GO-TO** *Recipes*

Darwin Cups

Denise Webb
Newington, GA

*These are my go-to favorite appetizers. Our friend Darwin
liked them so much that we named them for him.
The rest is history! I'm sure you will love them, too.*

8 slices bacon
10-oz. tube refrigerated
   flaky biscuits
3/4 c. shredded Swiss cheese
1/2 c. mayonnaise

3/4 c. ripe tomato, coarsely
   chopped
1/4 c. onion, coarsely chopped
1 t. dried basil

Cook bacon in a skillet over medium heat until crisp; drain well and
chop coarsely. Meanwhile, separate each biscuit horizontally into
3 thinner biscuits. Press each biscuit piece into a mini muffin cup, using
a mini tart shaper if desired; set aside. In a bowl, combine bacon and
remaining ingredients. Mix well; spoon mixture into biscuit cups. Bake
at 375 degrees for 10 to 12 minutes, until golden and cheese is melted.
Makes 2-1/2 dozen.

Find a reason to celebrate! Kids love it when you make a fuss
over their achievements, like a game-winning goal, an A in
math or a new Scout badge.

Tasty Treats ANYTIME

Tortellini & Pesto Dip

Barb Fulton
Arvada, CO

*Whenever I need a dish to bring to a potluck or gathering, this is a
great one! It's a little more than chips and it's not dessert. We also
like to use the dip to fill multicolored little mini sweet peppers. For a
yummy variation, use crumbled goat cheese instead of cream cheese.*

2 9-oz. pkgs. refrigerated cheese
   tortellini, uncooked
7-oz. jar basil pesto sauce

8-oz. pkg. cream cheese,
   softened
1 t. lemon juice

Cook tortellini according to package directions; drain and cool.
Meanwhile, in a bowl, mix together pesto, cream cheese and lemon
juice. Chill dip and tortellini separately. Serve tortellini alongside dip.
Serves 10 to 12.

Avocado Feta Dip

Anne Alesauskas
Minocqua, WI

*My family doesn't care for tomatoes but we love red peppers.
So I just substituted them for the tomatoes in this recipe.*

2 avocados, halved, pitted
   and diced
3/4 c. crumbled feta cheese
1 red pepper, diced
1 green onion, thinly sliced

1 T. lemon juice
2 t. dill weed
1/4 t. salt
1/4 t. pepper

Combine all ingredients in a serving bowl; mix until well blended.
Makes 3 cups, serves 12.

A quick and tasty appetizer in a jiffy! Place a block of cream cheese
on a serving plate, spoon sweet-hot pepper jelly over it
and serve with crunchy crackers.

Mom's GO-TO *Recipes*

Hidden Treasures

Amy Thomason Hunt
Traphill, NC

These are like the all-time favorite cocktail weenies everyone loves
at get-togethers, but they're a nice change of pace.

2 8-oz. tubes refrigerated
   crescent rolls
16 frozen meatballs, thawed

1 c. grated Parmesan cheese
Optional: favorite dipping sauce

Separate crescents; cut each into 2 triangles. Place a meatball on each
crescent and roll up, starting with a short end. Sprinkle with cheese;
place on an ungreased baking sheet. Bake at 400 degrees for 12 to
15 minutes, until hot and golden. Serve with dipping sauce, if desired.
Makes 8 servings, 2 each.

Pepperoni Biscuit Snacks

Gladys Brehm
Quakertown, PA

A nice little treat...the kids can help make these.

1 c. shredded mozzarella cheese
1/2 c. pepperoni, diced
1/2 c. pizza sauce

2 10-oz. tubes refrigerated
   biscuits
1 T. milk

In a bowl, combine cheese, pepperoni and pizza sauce; set aside.
Separate biscuits; flatten each into a 3-inch circle. Place one tablespoon
filling in the center of each biscuit; fold biscuit in half and pinch edges
to seal. Arrange on a lightly greased baking sheet; brush biscuits with
milk. Bake at 350 degrees for 12 to 15 minutes, until golden. Makes
20 pieces.

Need a quick, good-for-you after-school
snack for the kids? Serve up an old
favorite, Ants on a Log...celery sticks
filled with peanut butter and sprinkled
with raisins. Tasty and fun!

Tasty Treats
ANYTIME

Delicious Crabmeat English Muffins

Alain Santilli
Shelton, CT

My mom used to make these for us on New Year's Eve. I remember they were one of my favorites and I looked forward to them. Now I make them for my kids. I just freeze them and the kids can put them in the toaster oven for a snack anytime.

6-oz. can crabmeat, drained
   and flaked
5-oz. jar sharp pasteurized
   process cheese spread

1/2 c. butter, softened
1 t. seasoned salt
6 English muffins, split

In a bowl, combine all ingredients except muffins; mix well. Spread mixture on cut sides of muffin halves. Cut each muffin half into 8 wedges; arrange on a baking sheet. Broil until bubbly and lightly golden. May be frozen unbaked on a baking sheet, then stored in a plastic freezer bag; bake while still frozen. Makes 8 dozen.

Sweet or savory treats won't stick to baking sheets
lined with parchment paper. Clean-up is a snap too...
just toss away the paper.

Mom's GO-TO Recipes

Baked Zucchini Sticks

Cynthia Dodge
Queen Creek, AZ

This is a quick and nutritious way to get your family to eat more vegetables. Plus, it's a good way to use up all of that zucchini your neighbors leave on your doorstep! Works great with yellow summer squash also.

3 small to medium zucchini,
   ends trimmed
1 c. Italian-flavored dry bread
   crumbs

1/4 t. garlic powder
1/4 t. onion powder
2 egg whites, beaten
Garnish: ranch salad dressing

Cut zucchini into sticks, 2 to 3 inches long and about 1/4-inch thick; set aside. In a large bowl, mix together bread crumbs and spices; set aside. In a separate bowl, beat egg whites with an electric mixer on high setting until soft peaks form. Roll zucchini sticks in egg whites to coat well. Roll sticks into bread crumb mixture; place on lightly greased baking sheets. Bake at 425 degrees for 8 to 10 minutes, until lightly golden. Serve warm with a favorite dipping sauce or salad dressing.

Hosting a party? A 2 or 3-tier pie server is terrific for serving bite-size appetizers. It holds a lot, yet takes up little room on the buffet table.

Tasty Treats
ANYTIME

Calico Corn Salsa

Bonnie Weber
West Palm Beach, FL

This salsa is so pretty and goes well with almost anything. I serve it with tortilla chips for parties but it makes a great salsa for meat too.

2 15-oz. cans corn, drained
2 16-oz. cans black beans,
   drained and rinsed
1 green pepper, diced
1 onion, diced
1 bunch arugula, torn

6-oz. can black olives, drained
   and chopped
1 tomato, chopped
8-oz. bottle Italian salad dressing
salt and pepper to taste

In a large bowl, combine all ingredients; cover and refrigerate until chilled. Toss mixture gently before serving. Serves 8 to 10.

Serve up colorful salsa in mini canning jars. Tortilla chips
and veggie slices are easy to dip right into the jars...
and everyone gets their own jar!

Mom's GO-TO *Recipes*

Chili Cheese Dip

Lori Robb
Spring Creek, NV

As a young mom, I used to meet with other young moms once a month at one of our homes to share food, recipes, child-rearing tips, visiting and playing games. This recipe was easy and always a hit. And since I was a busy mom, it was easily put together when I was short on time. Enjoy and watch it disappear!

8-oz. pkg. cream cheese,
   softened
15-oz. can chili
8-oz. jar favorite salsa

1 c. shredded Cheddar cheese
2 to 3 T. sliced black olives
tortilla chips

Spread softened cream cheese in the bottom of an ungreased 9"x9" glass pie plate. Spread chili over cream cheese; spoon salsa over chili. Top with cheese and olives. Bake, uncovered, at 350 degrees for 30 minutes, until bubbly and cheese is melted. May also microwave on high for 10 minutes. Serve with tortilla chips. Makes 10 servings.

Make tonight a family game night! Get out all your favorite board games and play to your heart's content. Small prizes for winners and bowls of munchies are a must!

Tasty Treats
ANYTIME

Chip Chicken Lollipops

Barb Rudyk
Alberta, Canada

*This is a fun recipe for a children's party...but even adults
love it! I like to experiment with different flavors of
seasoned potato chips.*

1 egg, beaten
2 T. milk
2 c. potato chips, crushed
4 boneless, skinless chicken
    breasts, cubed

mini wooden skewers
Garnish: favorite dipping sauce

In a shallow bowl, whisk together egg and milk. Spread crushed potato
chips in a separate bowl. Dip chicken cubes into egg mixture; coat well
with potato chips. Arrange cubes onto a greased baking sheet. Bake at
350 degrees for 10 minutes; turn over. Bake for 10 minutes more, or
until golden. Remove baking sheet from oven and insert a skewer into
each chicken cube. Serve hot with dipping sauce. Makes 10 servings.

To keep party beverages from watering down, freeze iced tea
or lemonade in ice cube trays (or even mini muffin pans!)
and use instead of ordinary ice.

Virginia's Taco Dip

Karen Hallett
Nova Scotia, Canada

My sister Virginia gave me this recipe many years ago and it's been a family favorite ever since. Whenever we're having a get-together, I'm "told" that this is what I will be bringing. It is always a hit and I always go home with a clean dish!

1 lb. lean ground beef
8-oz. can tomato sauce
2 to 4 T. taco seasoning mix
8-oz. pkg. cream cheese,
  softened
3/4 c. mayonnaise

1 c. sour cream
Garnish: shredded lettuce,
  diced tomatoes, diced
  onions, shredded marble or
  mozzarella cheese
taco-flavored tortilla chips

Brown beef in a skillet over medium heat; drain. Stir in tomato sauce and desired amount of seasoning mix; remove from heat and allow to cool completely. Meanwhile, in a large bowl, beat cream cheese until soft. Add mayonnaise and sour cream; beat until well mixed. Spread cream cheese mixture evenly in 2 ungreased 13"x9" glass baking pans. Cover and refrigerate for about 30 minutes. Spread beef mixture over cream cheese layer in both pans; layer with desired toppings. Cover and refrigerate for several hours or overnight; the taco flavor will intensify. Serve with tortilla chips for dipping. Makes 2 pans, 12 servings each.

Whip up a creamy, sweet and spicy fruit dip. Blend 2 cups whipped topping with 1/4 cup brown sugar, 1/4 teaspoon cinnamon and 1/8 teaspoon nutmeg. Serve with a platter of sliced ripe fruit.

Tasty Treats
ANYTIME

Easy Mexican Chicken Dip

Connie Ramsey
Pontotoc, MS

This is quick, easy and a hearty treat that my whole family enjoys!

2 8-oz. pkgs. cream cheese,
   softened
2 12-1/2 oz. cans canned
   chicken, drained and flaked

16-oz. jar favorite salsa
8-oz. pkg. shredded Monterey
   Jack cheese
tortilla chips

Pat cream cheese into the bottom of a 13"x9" glass baking pan sprayed with non-stick vegetable spray. Spread chicken over cream cheese. Spoon salsa evenly over chicken; sprinkle with cheese. Bake, uncovered, at 350 degrees for about 20 minutes, until hot and bubbly. Serve warm with tortilla chips. Makes 6 to 8 servings.

Pickle-icious Dip

Kadie Davis
Saint Peter, MN

This is so easy and is always the first dip to go at our family buffets.
I got this recipe from a friend and it has become a family favorite!
If you like ham & pickle roll-ups, you will love this dip.

8-oz. pkg. cream cheese,
   softened
1 c. mayonnaise
2 2-oz. pkgs. deli baked ham,
   finely chopped

1 c. dill pickle relish, plus 1 to
   2 T. juice from relish
shredded wheat crackers or other
   snack crackers

Combine all ingredients except crackers in a large bowl; mix well. Pickle flavor may be adjusted by adding more or less of the relish or pickle juice. Cover and chill for several hours or overnight. Serve with crackers. Makes 12 servings.

Soften cream cheese in a hurry! Place an unwrapped 8-ounce block on a plate and microwave at 50% power for about one minute.

Mom's GO-TO *Recipes*

Dippy Cauliflower

Judy Lange
Imperial, PA

A fast and easy appetizer that everyone enjoys!

1 head cauliflower, cut into
　bite-size flowerets
3 T. water
1/2 c. butter, melted

1 c. Italian-flavored dry
　bread crumbs
1 c. shredded Cheddar cheese

In a microwave-safe dish, combine cauliflower and water. Cover with plastic wrap; microwave on high for 5 minutes. Drain. Dip each floweret into melted butter; roll in bread crumbs. Arrange in a greased 13"x9" baking pan. Bake, uncovered, at 375 degrees for about 20 minutes, until tender and golden. Remove from oven; sprinkle with cheese. Return to oven until cheese melts, about 5 minutes. Makes 6 servings.

Homemade buttermilk dressing is wonderful on salads...
it's a delicious dip for veggies too! Blend 1/2 cup mayonnaise,
1/2 cup buttermilk, one teaspoon dried parsley, 1/2 teaspoon onion
powder, 1/4 teaspoon garlic powder, 1/8 teaspoon dill weed and
a little salt and pepper. Keep refrigerated.

Tasty Treats
ANYTIME

Ranch Ham & Tortilla Pinwheels
Lisa Johnson
Hallsville, TX

These are a favorite of all ages...after school,
after work or just because!

1 c. deli smoked ham, cubed
2 8-oz. pkgs. cream cheese,
　softened
0.4-oz. pkg. ranch salad
　dressing mix

2 green onions, minced
14 12-inch flour tortillas
4-oz. can diced green chiles
Optional: 2-1/4 oz. can sliced
　black olives, drained

Mix together ham, cream cheese, ranch dressing mix and green onions in a bowl; spread on tortillas. Sprinkle with chiles and olives, if desired. Roll tortillas tightly. Chill 2 hours or up to 24 hours. Slice rolls into one-inch pieces. Makes 3 dozen.

Irene's Herbed Cheese
Irene Robinson
Cincinnati, OH

This cheese spread is delicious and it can be whipped up in
a moment. The seasoning can be adjusted to suit your taste.

8-oz. pkg. cream cheese,
　softened
2 cloves garlic, pressed

1 T. fines herbes seasoning
Garnish: chopped fresh parsley
assorted crackers

In a food processor, combine cream cheese, garlic and seasoning; process until blended. Cover and chill overnight. To serve, form into a ball; roll in chopped parsley. Serve with crackers. Makes one cup.

Oh-so-easy iced tea...fill up a 2-quart pitcher with water and drop in 6 to 8 tea bags. Refrigerate overnight. Discard tea bags, sweeten to taste and serve over ice.

Mom's GO-TO *Recipes*

Black Bean & Avocado Salsa
*Mignonne Gardner
Pleasant Grove, UT*

*Nothing says "fresh from the garden" like a bowl full of
colorful vegetables! This is the perfect salsa. It's mild,
yet delicious and full of flavor.*

2 15-1/2 oz. cans black beans,
   drained and rinsed
2 avocados, peeled, pitted
   and diced
2 roma tomatoes, chopped

1 c. frozen corn, thawed
6 green onions, thinly sliced
1/2 c. fresh cilantro, chopped
pepper to taste
tortilla chips

Combine all ingredients except tortilla chips in a large bowl; mix well.
Drizzle with Lime Dressing; stir to coat mixture with dressing. Cover and
chill until serving time. Serve with tortilla chips. Serves 4 to 6.

Lime Dressing:

1/3 c. fresh lime juice
1/2 c. olive oil
1 clove garlic, minced

1 to 2 t. salt
1/8 t. cayenne pepper

Combine all ingredients in a small bowl; whisk until combined.

Mashed avocado can be frozen for quick guacamole. Just add
1/2 teaspoon of lime or lemon juice per avocado, mix well, and store
in a plastic zipping bag, making sure to press out all the air before
sealing. To use, thaw in the refrigerator.

Tasty Treats
ANYTIME

Hummus Ranch Dip

Liz Plotnick-Snay
Gooseberry Patch

I love being able to whip up this tasty, healthy dip in a moment whenever we want a snack. If it's for a get-together, I'll make a double batch.

15-oz. can garbanzo beans,
   rinsed and drained
1/4 c. ranch salad dressing
3 T. warm water

1 T. lemon juice
1 clove garlic, chopped
red pepper strips, baby carrots,
   pita chips

In a food processor or blender, combine beans, salad dressing, water, lemon juice and garlic. Process until smooth. Serve immediately, or cover and chill. Serve as a dip with pepper strips, carrots and pita wedges. Makes 4 servings.

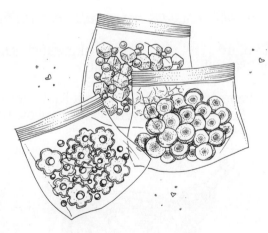

Colorful fresh vegetables are always welcome at parties and easy to prepare in advance. Cut them into bite-size slices, flowerets or cubes and tuck away in plastic zipping bags until needed...what a time-saver!

Mom's GO-TO *Recipes*

Ranch Cheese Ball

Sophia Collins
McHenry, MS

This is a quick recipe that I use whenever we have gatherings at church or work.

2 8-oz. pkgs. cream cheese,
  softened
1-oz. pkg. ranch salad
  dressing mix

3 green onions, chopped
13-oz. pkg. round buttery
  crackers, divided

In a large bowl, blend cream cheese, dressing mix and onions. Scoop onto plastic wrap; shape into a ball and refrigerate for at least 2 to 4 hours. Before serving, crush 6 to 7 crackers; roll ball in crushed crackers. Serve with remaining crackers. Serves 15 to 20.

Low-Fat Homemade Ranch Dressing

Lisa Langston
Conroe, TX

This is delish and oh-so easy! Serve on salad or with fresh veggies.

1 c. plain Greek yogurt
1/2 c. fat-free or 2% milk

1-oz. pkg. ranch salad dressing
  mix

Combine all ingredients in a canning jar with a lid. Cover and shake until well blended. Refrigerate for several hours to allow flavors to blend. Makes 1-1/2 cups.

Keep a bowl of creamy dip cool and tasty...nestle it inside a larger bowl filled with crushed ice.

Tasty Treats
ANYTIME

Ham Roll-Ups

Robin Crane
Elyria, OH

Mom always made these for family get-togethers. These may sound too easy to be so good, but believe me...people just pop them into their mouths! These are best when made the day before.

2 8-oz. pkgs cream cheese,
    room temperature
Optional: 1 to 2 T. onion,
    finely chopped

16-oz. pkg. sliced deli chopped
    ham

Place cream cheese in a bowl. Add desired amount of onion; stir together. Spread some of cheese mixture on each slice of ham, all the way to the edges. Roll up each slice; place seam-side down on aluminum foil or plastic wrap. Refrigerate for 4 hours to overnight. At serving time, cut into 1/2-inch slices; fasten with toothpicks. Serves 12 to 15.

Wagon Wheels

Michelle Corriveau
Blackstone, MA

When we were kids, Mom always made these on New Year's Eve. So easy and so good!

16 slices deli Genoa salami

2 8-oz. pkgs. cream cheese,
    room temperature

Using 4 slices salami per stack, layer salami and cream cheese into stacks. Cut each stack into 6 wedges. Keep refrigerated. Serves 12.

Looking to save a few calories in your snacks? Replace regular cream cheese with the 1/3 less fat version.

Mom's GO-TO *Recipes*

Cheeseburger Cups

Lynn Williams
Muncie, IN

These yummy biscuit cups taste like your favorite burger!
My kids love them for parties, or just for supper.

1 lb. ground beef
10-1/2 oz. can French
   onion soup
2 T. catsup

5 slices American cheese, divided
12-oz. tube refrigerated biscuits
Garnish: shredded lettuce,
   tomato slices, dill pickle slices

Brown beef in a skillet over medium heat; drain. Stir in soup and catsup; simmer for 5 minutes. Add 2-1/2 slices cheese; cook and stir until cheese is melted. Meanwhile, flatten biscuits; press into the bottoms and up the sides of 10 greased muffin cups. Spoon 1/4 cup of beef mixture into each cup, mounding mixture in the center. Bake at 375 degrees for 15 minutes, or until biscuits are golden. Cut remaining cheese slices into quarters; place one piece on top of each cup. Let stand until cheese is melted; add desired toppings. Makes 10 servings.

For children's parties, bright-colored plastic Frisbees make great
no-spill holders for flimsy paper plates. After the party,
kids can take them home as an extra party favor.

Tasty Treats
ANYTIME

Corn Dog Mini Muffins

Mary Patenaude
Griswold, CT

These make great party appetizers, or serve with
soup or salad for a quick lunch.

8-1/2 oz. pkg. corn muffin mix
1 egg, beaten
1/3 c. milk
1 T. honey mustard

4 hot dogs, cut into
   1/2-inch pieces
1/2 c. shredded Cheddar
   cheese

In a large bowl, stir together muffin mix, egg, milk and mustard. Fold in hot dog pieces and cheese. Drop batter by tablespoonfuls into 32 lightly greased muffin cups. Bake at 350 degrees for 10 to 15 minutes, until lightly golden. Cool in pan on a wire rack for 5 minutes; turn muffins out of pan. Makes about 2-1/2 dozen.

Mud Soda

Jill Ball
Highland, UT

My children always loved this treat when they were little.
Kids can't resist something called a mud soda!

2 c. chocolate milk, chilled
2 c. root beer, chilled

1 c. chocolate ice cream

To each of 4 tall glasses, add 1/2 cup milk and 1/2 cup root beer; stir gently to mix. Top each serving with 1/4 cup ice cream. Serve with a straw and a long spoon. Makes 4 servings.

'Tis the sweet, simple things of life which are the real ones after all.

– Laura Ingalls Wilder

Barbecue Snack Mix

Shannon Reents
Bellville, OH

Great for munching on while watching your favorite football game,
or pack it up to take to high school games or picnics.

3 c. bite-size corn rice cereal
3 c. bite-size Cheddar cheese
   crackers
2 c. oyster crackers
2 c. mini pretzel twists
Optional: 1 c. whole almonds

6 T. butter, melted
2 T. barbecue seasoning mix
1 T. brown sugar, packed
1 T. cider vinegar
1 t. Worcestershire sauce

In a large bowl, combine cereal, crackers, pretzels and almonds, if using;
toss to mix and set aside. In a separate bowl, combine remaining
ingredients; mix well. Pour evenly over cereal mixture; stir gently until
well coated. Spread on ungreased baking sheets. Bake at 250 degrees
for 45 minutes, stirring every 15 minutes. Pour out onto a large sheet
of parchment paper; allow to cool. Store in an airtight container at room
temperature. Makes 9 cups.

White paper coffee filters make tidy toss-away holders
for servings of popcorn and snack mix. Pick up
a big package at a dollar store!

Tasty Treats ANYTIME

Strawberry Preserves Smoothies

Etha Hutchcroft
Ames, IA

Serve this farm-fresh breakfast smoothie in small canning jars with a pretty straw for a fun presentation.

2 T. strawberry preserves
1 c. crushed pineapple
1 c. orange juice
3 c. fresh strawberries, hulled
    and sliced

8-oz. container strawberry
    yogurt
8-oz. container plain yogurt

Combine all ingredients in a blender; process until smooth. Pour into chilled jelly jars to serve. Makes 4 servings.

Peanut Butter-Banana Smoothies

Jennifer Levy
Warners, NY

This recipe makes the most delicious, satisfying smoothies. They're healthy, and kids love them! Add a scoop of chocolate protein powder for an extra boost.

2 c. unsweetened vanilla
    almond milk
2 ripe bananas, sliced

1/3 c. creamy peanut butter
2 T. honey
5 ice cubes

Add all ingredients to a blender; process until smooth. Pour into 2 tall glasses. Makes 2 servings.

Looking for an alternative to peanut butter? Try sun butter, made from sunflower seeds, or soy nut butter, made from soybeans. Check with your child's doctor first in case of peanut allergy.

Mom's GO-TO Recipes

PB&J Bananas

Courtney Stultz
Weir, KS

My kids love helping in the kitchen. I love to give them easy, healthy recipes to make themselves. For this simple snack, they can choose what ingredients they want for themselves...no cooking required!

1 ripe banana, split in half
   lengthwise
1 to 2 t. creamy peanut or
   almond butter

1 t. strawberry jam
Optional: flaked coconut,
   chocolate chips, chopped
   nuts or raisins

Spread banana halves with peanut butter and jam. Add optional toppings, if desired. Makes 2 servings.

Apple-licious Bagels

Julie Dossantos
Fort Pierce, FL

One of our favorite snacks is apple slices dipped in peanut butter. This gave us a great idea for a delicious bagel topping!

1 Gala apple, cored and diced
1 t. cinnamon
2 T. creamy peanut butter

2 whole-wheat bagels, split
   and toasted

Combine apple and cinnamon in a small bowl; set aside. Spread peanut butter on bagel halves; top with apple mixture. Serves 2.

The safe way to slice a bagel! Place it on a cutting board and cut in half, then place each half, flat-side down, and slice through, top to bottom.

Tasty Treats
ANYTIME

Healthy Moon Balls

Pat Martin
Riverside, CA

*I've made these healthy treats for over 30 years, first for my sons
who are now in their forties, and now for my two grandchildren.
They're so tasty, I also make them for my husband and myself!*

1/2 c. creamy peanut butter	1 c. non-fat dry milk powder
1/2 c. honey	1 c. graham cracker crumbs

Mix peanut butter and honey in a bowl. Gradually add milk powder;
mix well. Roll into one-inch balls; roll in graham cracker crumbs. Chill.
Makes 5 dozen.

Creamy Yogurt Apple Dip

Anna McMaster
Portland, OR

The kids love this speedy dip as an after-school treat.

8-oz. container plain	1 T. honey
Greek yogurt	1/4 t. cinnamon
2 to 2-1/2 T. creamy	apple wedges or slices
peanut butter	

In a bowl, combine all ingredients except apples; cover and chill. Serve
with apple wedges. Serves 4.

Keep sliced apples in the fridge for snacking later today. Combine
one cup water and 2 tablespoons honey. Add apple slices, soak for
30 seconds and drain. No browning!

173

Mom's GO-TO Recipes

Sweet Little Piggies

Peggy Dollens
Bargersville, IN

*My girls loved these as teenagers...my husband
likes them too. Yummy!*

1/2 c. butter, melted
6 T. honey
6 T. brown sugar, packed
1-1/2 c. chopped pecans

8-oz. tube refrigerated
   crescent rolls
24 mini smoked sausages

Spread melted butter in a 13"x9" baking pan. Pour honey over melted butter; sprinkle brown sugar over top and stir around in pan to distribute evenly. Sprinkle with pecans; set aside. Cut each crescent roll into 3 triangles. Place one sausage on the shortest side of each triangle; roll up. Arrange in pan, point-side down. Bake at 400 degrees for 15 to 20 minutes, until crescent rolls are lightly golden. Makes 2 dozen.

When measuring sticky ingredients like honey or maple syrup,
spray the measuring cup with non-stick vegetable spray first.
The contents will slip right out and you'll get a more
accurate measurement.

Tasty Treats
ANYTIME

Pizza-Style Nachos

Lisa Ann Panzino DiNunzio
Vineland, NJ

*A delicious, easy and fun take on pizza that you can serve
at a family get-together or as a snack.*

13-oz. pkg. tortilla chips
1-1/2 c. favorite pizza or
   pasta sauce
3 T. shredded Parmesan cheese

8-oz. pkg. shredded mozzarella
   or pizza-blend cheese
1 t. dried oregano

Spread tortilla chips evenly on a 15"x10" jelly-roll pan coated with
non-stick vegetable spray. Lightly spoon sauce over tortilla chips; don't
saturate. Sprinkle with cheeses and oregano. Bake at 375 degrees for
10 to 15 minutes, until cheese is melted. Serve immediately. Makes
4 to 6 servings.

Kids 8 and up love make-your-own bars. Set up all
the fixings for pizza, tacos or ice cream sundaes and
let 'em do it themselves!

Baked Chicken Wings

Nancy Wise
Little Rock, AR

My family loves these tasty wings...so do my guests! Sometimes I'll add a dash of cayenne pepper for a spicy kick. Best of all, there's no messy frying.

1 c. grated Parmesan cheese	1/8 t. salt
1 c. seasoned dry bread crumbs	1/8 t. pepper
1/8 t. garlic powder	5 lbs. chicken wings, separated
1/8 t. onion powder	1/2 c. butter, melted

Line baking sheets with aluminum foil; add a wire rack. Spray well with non-stick vegetable spray. In a bowl, combine Parmesan cheese, bread crumbs and seasonings. Dip chicken wings into melted butter; press into bread crumb mixture until well-coated. Arrange wings on baking sheets. Bake at 400 degrees for 20 to 25 minutes. Flip chicken wings and continue baking another 20 to 25 minutes, until golden and no longer pink in the center. Serves 20.

A tray of warm, moistened towels is a nice touch when serving sticky finger foods! Dampen fingertip towels in water and a dash of lemon juice, roll up and microwave on high for 10 to 15 seconds.

Tasty Treats
ANYTIME

Buffalo Chicken Cheese Dip
Rhonda McCormick
Morehead, KY

This dip is much too good to only serve once a year! One of my teenage daughter's friends brought this to our house for a tailgating party several years ago. We had chips, crackers and veggies to go with the dip, but the boys just dug in with spoons!

4 boneless, skinless chicken
   breasts, cooked and shredded
8-oz. pkg. cream cheese,
   softened
1/2 c. crumbled blue cheese
8-oz. bottle blue cheese salad
   dressing

1 c. favorite hot wing sauce
8-oz. pkg. finely shredded mild
   or sharp Cheddar cheese
tortilla chips, crackers, celery and
   other fresh vegetables

In a large bowl, combine chicken, cream cheese, blue cheese, salad dressing and wing sauce. Beat with an electric mixer on low speed until well blended. Transfer mixture to a 13"x9" baking pan lightly coated with non-stick vegetable spray. Cover with Cheddar cheese. Bake, uncovered, at 350 degrees for 20 minutes, or until heated through and cheese is melted. Serve with tortilla chips, crackers, celery and other assorted cut vegetables. Serves 25.

Whip up some tasty salsa for snacking in a jiffy! In a blender, combine a can of stewed or diced tomatoes, several slices of canned jalapeños and a teaspoon or 2 of the jalapeño juice. Cover and process to the desired consistency.

Mom's GO-TO *Recipes*

Party Mix for a Crowd

Pam Hooley
LaGrange, IN

I received some of this party mix for a gift. I liked it so much, I asked for the recipe! It's great for big gatherings and for gift-giving, because it makes so much. You can vary the ingredients with other kinds of cereals or snacks...I do every time, depending on what I have on hand.

12-oz. pkg. crispy corn & rice
    cereal squares
12-oz. pkg. crispy rice cereal
    squares
12-oz. pkg. mini pretzel twists
12-oz. pkg. baked cheese
    snack crackers

8-oz. pkg. horn-shaped corn
    snacks
2 16-oz. cans mixed nuts
2 c. butter-flavored popcorn oil
2 1-oz. pkgs. ranch salad
    dressing mix

In a very large roaster pan, combine all ingredients except oil and salad dressing mix. Mix well; set aside. In a bowl, stir together oil and dressing mix; pour over cereal mixture and mix very well. Spread on ungreased baking sheets. Bake at 250 degrees for 30 to 60 minutes, stirring occasionally, until mixture is as golden as desired. Cool; store in an airtight container. Makes 15 to 20 servings.

Peanuts are yummy in crunchy snack mixes, but if you need to avoid them, there are tasty substitutes to try! Choose from raisins, sweetened dried cranberries, dried fruit bits, candy-coated chocolates, chocolate chips and even mini pretzel twists.

Tasty Treats
ANYTIME

Road Trip Trail Mix

Betty Lou Wright
Fort Worth, TX

When we lived in Tennessee, this trail mix saved the day on long trips to Texas to visit our son. The combination of salty and sweet is delicious! I shared the recipe with my friend Ann in Georgia, and it quickly became a keeper for her family too. It's easily doubled.

16-oz. pkg. dry-roasted
    salted peanuts
16-oz. pkg. salted cashews

8-oz. pkg. raisins
8-oz. pkg. candy-coated
    chocolates

Combine all ingredients in a large bowl; mix well. Store in an airtight container. Makes about 9 cups.

Cinnamon Pretzels

Meri Hebert
Cheboygan, MI

This is very easy recipe to make...great for the busy holiday season or for snacking anytime. I like to make several batches to pack in small treat bags for gifts.

2/3 c. oil
1/2 c. sugar

2 t. cinnamon
16-oz. pkg. mini pretzel twists

In a large roasting pan, stir together oil, sugar and cinnamon. Add pretzels; toss well to combine. Bake, uncovered, at 300 degrees for 30 minutes, stirring twice. Spread on wax paper to cool. Store in an airtight container. Makes 12 cups.

Save the plastic liners from cereal boxes. They're perfect for storing homemade snack mixes.

Veggie Dip

Tori Mason
Nashville, TN

This has been a family recipe for as long as I can remember. My mom always brought it to family gatherings...if for some odd reason she didn't bring it, everyone got upset! My little cousin Ronnie dubbed it "Aunt Jan's Carrot Dip" when he was about 5 years old. He is now grown up and married, with a son of his own, and it's his son's favorite now too! When I bring it to get-togethers with friends, it's always a hit.

8-oz. pkg cream cheese, softened
8-oz. container sour cream
1 T. catsup
1 T. Worcestershire Sauce
1/8 t. onion powder

1-oz. pkg. vegetable soup mix
sliced vegetables such as carrots,
   celery, cucumber, broccoli,
   peppers

In a large bowl, beat cream cheese with an electric mixer on low speed until light and fluffy. Beat in sour cream until well blended. Stir in catsup, Worcestershire sauce, onion powder and soup mix. Transfer to an airtight container; cover and refrigerate for several hours to allow flavors to blend. Serve with sliced vegetables. Makes 15 servings.

Planning a big party? Borrow seldom-used party items like folding tables, punch bowls or a chocolate fountain from a friend or neighbor. Most people are happy to share!

Tasty Treats
ANYTIME

One-Pot Chili Dip

Victoria Mitchel
Gettysburg, PA

This is a super-easy last-minute appetizer! I came up with this when I had some leftover homemade chili...put it in a pan, added a little of this & that, and came up with a winner. Enjoy!

15-oz. can chili, or
   1-1/2 c. homemade chili
10-oz. can diced tomatoes with
   green chiles

8-oz. pkg cream cheese, cubed
1 c. shredded Mexican-blend
   cheese
tortilla chips

Combine chili, tomatoes with juice and cream cheese in a saucepan. Cook over low heat, stirring often, until cream cheese melts and all is blended. Add shredded cheese; cook and stir until melted and heated through. Serve warm with tortilla chips. For a party, keep warm in a slow cooker set on low. Serves 6 to 8.

A festive container for chips in a jiffy! Simply tie a knot
in each corner of a brightly colored bandanna,
then tuck a bowl into the center.

181

Mom's GO-TO Recipes

Candy Sprinkles Cheesecake Ball

Audra Vanhorn-Sorey
Columbia, NC

A sweet and easy treat that's a birthday cake lover's dream!

8-oz. pkg cream cheese, softened
1/2 c. butter, softened
1-1/2 c. cake mix with candy
   sprinkles

1/2 c. powdered sugar
3 T. sugar
1/2 c. rainbow candy sprinkles
vanilla wafers, graham crackers

In a large bowl, beat cream cheese and butter together until combined. Add dry cake mix and sugars; stir until combined. Scoop mixture onto a large piece of plastic wrap; form into a ball. Wrap and freeze for 90 minutes, or until firm enough to hold its shape. Pour candy sprinkles into a bowl. Unwrap cheese ball; roll in sprinkles until completely covered. Place on a serving dish; serve with vanilla wafers or graham crackers. Serves 12 to 20.

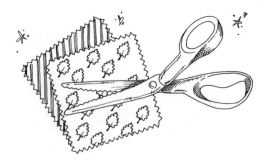

Want a special tablecloth for a party buffet? There are so many charming print fabrics available at fabric stores. Two to three yards is all you'll need. No hemming required...just trim the edges with pinking shears!

Mom's Best
DESSERTS

Mom's GO-TO *Recipes*

Virginia Brownies

Suzanne Varnes
Toccoa, GA

This recipe makes a fudgy, dense brownie that's good with or without the glaze. It's based on a recipe my mom made often when my brother and I were kids. Once we were old enough to make them on our own, we would set up a brownie stand in lieu of the usual lemonade stand! May be halved to make in an 8-inch square pan.

1-1/2 c. all-purpose flour
2 c. sugar
1/2 c. plus 1 t. baking cocoa
1 t. salt

4 eggs, beaten
1 t. vanilla extract
Optional: 1 c. chopped nuts
    or chocolate chips

Combine all ingredients in a large bowl; mix well. Spread batter in a greased 13"x9" baking pan. Bake at 350 degrees for 30 minutes. Pour hot Glaze over hot brownies. Cool to room temperature before cutting into squares. Makes 2 to 3 dozen.

Glaze:

1 c. sugar
1/4 c. baking cocoa
1/4 c. whipping cream or
    whole milk

1-1/2 T. butter
1 t. vanilla extract

Combine sugar, cocoa and cream or milk in a saucepan; bring to a rolling boil. Boil, stirring constantly, for 2 minutes. Remove from heat. Add butter and vanilla; stir until slightly thickened and butter has melted.

Serve brownie sundaes for a special treat. Place brownies on individual dessert plates and top with a scoop of ice cream, a drizzle of chocolate syrup, a dollop of whipped cream and a maraschino cherry. Yummy!

Mom's Best
DESSERTS

Fudgy Choco-Toffee Bars

Katie Majeske
Denver, PA

A few years ago, my daughter made a pan of these when she was home from college. We knew it wouldn't be the last time! They are a go-to whenever we need sweets.

30-oz. tube refrigerated chocolate chip cookie dough
1/2 c. plus 1 T. butter, melted and divided
2 c. graham cracker crumbs, divided

8-oz. pkg. toffee bits, divided
14-oz. can sweetened condensed milk
12-oz. pkg. semi-sweet chocolate chips
1 t. vanilla extract

Let cookie dough stand at room temperature for about 10 minutes. Meanwhile, in a bowl, mix together 1/2 cup melted butter, 1-1/2 cups graham cracker crumbs and 3/4 cup toffee bits. Press into a greased 13"x9" baking pan; cover and refrigerate for 15 minutes. In a saucepan over medium heat, combine condensed milk, chocolate chips and remaining butter. Cook and stir until chips are melted and mixture is smooth. Remove from heat; stir in vanilla. Spread mixture over graham cracker crust; set aside. In a separate large bowl, break up cookie dough; add remaining graham cracker crumbs and mix until blended. Crumble mixture over chocolate layer; sprinkle with remaining toffee bits. Bake at 350 degrees for 25 to 35 minutes, until golden. Cool completely before cutting into squares. Makes 2 to 3 dozen.

Baking together is such a fun family activity. As you measure and mix together, be sure to share any stories about hand-me-down recipes...you'll be creating memories as well as sweet treats!

185

Mom's GO-TO Recipes

Grandma's Sugar Cookies

Jan Purnell
Littlestown, PA

My grandmother lived with us for several years and she did all of the cooking. What I treasure most are the memories of her in the kitchen at Christmas, when she would create the most wonderful treats. These sugar cookies are a family favorite...they bring back so many fond memories of her.

1 c. shortening
2 c. sugar
2 eggs, beaten
2 t. vanilla extract
4 c. all-purpose flour

1 t. baking soda
1 t. cream of tartar
1 c. buttermilk
Garnish: white or colored sugar

In a large bowl, blend shortening, sugar, eggs and vanilla; set aside. Into a separate bowl, sift flour, baking soda and cream of tartar. Add flour mixture to shortening mixture alternately with buttermilk; mix well. Drop dough by tablespoons onto greased baking sheets. Sprinkle with sugar as desired. Bake at 350 degrees for 6 to 8 minutes, until golden. Makes about 3 dozen.

Need a little colored sugar for cookies or cupcakes? Just place 1/4 cup sugar in a small jar, add a drop or 2 of food coloring, cover the jar and shake to blend well. Spread the sugar on wax paper and let it dry before using.

Mom's Best DESSERTS

Snickerdoodles

Hollie Moots
Marysville, OH

*A favorite cookie from my childhood. Now I love
making them for my family to enjoy too!*

2-3/4 c. all-purpose flour
2 t. baking powder
1/2 t. salt
1 c. butter, softened

1-3/4 c. sugar, divided
2 eggs, beaten
2 t. cinnamon

In a bowl, combine flour, baking powder and salt; set aside. Combine
butter and 1-1/2 cups sugar in a separate large bowl. Beat with an
electric mixer on medium speed until pale and fluffy. Stir in eggs;
gradually beat in flour mixture. Combine remaining sugar and cinnamon
in a small bowl. Shape dough into balls by teaspoonfuls; roll in
cinnamon-sugar. Arrange balls on parchment paper-lined baking sheets,
2 inches apart. Bake at 350 degrees for 12 to 15 minutes, until edges
are golden. Makes 2 dozen.

Gluten-Free Peanut Butter Blossom Cookies

Wendy Jo Minotte
Duluth, MN

*This is my go-to recipe whenever I am asked to provide cookies for
a bake sale. Only five ingredients and ready in one hour or less!
They taste great, and you'll never miss the flour.*

1 c. creamy peanut butter
1 c. sugar
1 egg, beaten

1 t. vanilla extract
30 milk chocolate drops,
    unwrapped

In a bowl, blend peanut butter and sugar. Add egg and vanilla; stir
until well mixed. Roll dough into one-inch balls. Arrange on ungreased
baking sheets, 2 inches apart. Bake at 350 degrees for 10 minutes, or
until tops are slightly cracked. Immediately press a chocolate drop into
the center of each cookie. Cool on baking sheets for 5 minutes; remove
to a wire rack and cool completely. Makes 2-1/2 dozen.

Grammy's Lemon Rounds

Sandra Smith
Lancaster, CA

These are a family favorite. Since the dough freezes well, I like to make up several batches at one time. My sons have grown up, so I often bake just a dozen cookies at a time for the two of us. During the holidays, I like to drizzle a little lemon glaze over the cookies.

1-1/2 c. all-purpose flour
1/2 t. baking soda
1/2 t. salt
1/2 c. shortening, softened
1 c. sugar

1 egg, beaten
1 T. lemon juice
2 t. lemon zest
1/2 c. finely chopped pecans

In a bowl, sift together flour, baking soda and salt; set aside. In a large bowl, blend shortening with sugar until fluffy; beat in egg, lemon juice, zest and pecans. Stir in flour mixture, blending well to make a soft dough. Shape dough into 2 long rolls; wrap in wax paper and chill overnight. When ready to bake, slice dough 1/4-inch thick; arrange on parchment paper-lined baking sheets. Bake at 375 degrees for 8 minutes, or until golden around the edges. Cool completely on wire racks. Makes 4 dozen.

For the tastiest results, reduce the oven temperature by 25 degrees if you're using glass or dark baking pans...they retain heat more than shiny pans do.

Mom's Best DESSERTS

Key Lime Bars

Vickie
Gooseberry Patch

A taste of the tropics! Perfect for summertime, yet equally welcome after a big holiday meal.

2-1/4 c. all-purpose flour,
   divided
2/3 c. powdered sugar
1 t. baking powder, divided

1 c. butter, softened
5 eggs, beaten
2 c. sugar
1/2 c. lime juice

In a bowl, combine 2 cups flour, powdered sugar and 1/2 teaspoon baking powder. Cut in butter with 2 forks until mixture resembles coarse crumbs. Press dough into a lightly greased 13"x9" baking pan. Bake at 350 degrees for 20 to 25 minutes, until lightly golden. Meanwhile, in another bowl, stir together eggs, sugar, lime juice and remaining flour and baking powder. Pour over hot crust. Return to oven; bake for another 22 to 25 minutes, until lightly golden. Cut into bars. Makes 2 dozen.

Use a sugar shaker to save clean-up time in the kitchen. It's ideal for dusting powdered sugar onto cookies and desserts still warm from the oven.

Mom's GO-TO *Recipes*

Scrumptious Chocolate Chip Cake

Carol Cousins
Dalworthington Gardens, TX

This cake is wonderful, but it isn't hard to make. Try not to eat this whole delicious cake by yourself!

3 c. all-purpose flour
1 t. baking powder
1/2 t. salt
1 c. butter, softened
2 c. sugar
1 T. vanilla extract

4 eggs
3/4 c. milk
12-oz. pkg. mini semi-sweet
   chocolate chips
Optional: powdered sugar,
   melted chocolate

Combine flour, baking powder and salt in a bowl; mix well and set aside. In a separate large bowl, combine butter, sugar and vanilla. Beat with an electric mixer on medium speed until creamy; beat in eggs, one at time. Gradually beat in flour mixture alternately with milk. Stir in chocolate chips. Pour batter into a greased and floured 10" Bundt® pan. Bake at 325 degrees for 70 to 80 minutes, until a toothpick inserted near center comes out clean. Cool cake in pan for 15 minutes; turn out onto a wire rack. Cool completely. Transfer cake to a cake plate; dust with powdered sugar or drizzle with melted chocolate. Serves 10 to 12.

Grease and flour cake pans in one easy step! Combine 1/2 cup shortening with 1/4 cup all-purpose flour. Keep this handy mix in a covered jar stored at room temperature.

Mom's Best DESSERTS

Banana Split Ice Cream Pie

Patsy Roberts
Center, TX

Good anytime! Easy to make ahead for a party another day.

2 ripe bananas, sliced
9-inch chocolate cookie crust
2 pts. strawberry ice cream,
  softened
20-oz. can crushed pineapple,
  drained

8-oz. container frozen whipped
  topping, thawed
1/4 c. chopped walnuts
  or almonds
Optional: maraschino cherries,
  drained

Arrange banana slices in the bottom of crust. Spread ice cream evenly
over bananas; top with pineapple. Spread whipped topping over
pineapple and sprinkle with nuts. Cover and freeze for 4 hours, or until
firm. At serving time, let stand for a few minutes before slicing. Top
with cherries, if desired. Makes 8 servings.

Make a luscious dessert topping to spoon over ice cream or
sliced pound cake...yum! Combine a cup of maple syrup and
a cup of toasted walnuts in a canning jar. Cover and store
at room temperature up to 2 weeks.

Mom's GO-TO *Recipes*

Hawaiian Bars

Linda Belon
Wintersville, OH

These cookie bars are very good! They're a favorite of my family.
We all like pineapple and Hawaiian-style foods. Stir in some
chopped macadamia nuts to make it extra special.

1/4 c. plus 1 T. margarine,
    divided
1 c. brown sugar, packed
1-1/2 c. flaked coconut
1 c. all-purpose flour

3/4 t. salt, divided
8-oz. can crushed pineapple
3/4 c. sugar
3 T. cornstarch
1 T. lemon juice

In a bowl, blend 1/4 cup margarine and brown sugar until light and
fluffy. Add coconut, flour and 1/2 teaspoon salt; mix with a fork until
crumbly. Press half of crumb mixture into a greased 9"x9" baking pan;
set aside. In a saucepan over medium heat, combine pineapple with
juice, sugar, cornstarch and remaining salt; stir to mix. Bring to a boil.
Cook, stirring constantly, for 5 minutes, or until thickened. Remove
from heat; stir in lemon juice and remaining margarine. Allow to cool
slightly; spread pineapple mixture evenly over crumb mixture. Cover
with remaining crumb mixture; gently press down. Bake at 350 degrees
for 30 to 35 minutes. Cut into squares. Makes one to 2 dozen.

For best results when baking, allow butter and eggs to come to
room temperature. Just set them out on the counter about an
hour ahead of time and they'll be ready.

Mom's Best DESSERTS

Mom's Crispy Rice Bars

*Diane Himpelmann
Ringwood, IL*

Every year, Mom made these bars for Christmas and Easter. She would wrap them individually in plastic wrap, and everyone who came to the house received a little bag of treats to take home. People always looked forward to her special treat.

6 c. crispy rice cereal	1 c. creamy peanut butter
1 c. mixed nuts or peanuts	25 caramels, unwrapped
1/2 c. butter	10-oz. pkg. mini marshmallows

Combine cereal and nuts in a greased large bowl; set aside. In a saucepan over medium-low heat, melt butter, peanut butter and caramels; stir in marshmallows. With a greased spoon, add marshmallow mixture to cereal mixture; stir to coat well. Press into a greased 13"x9" baking pan. Cool; cut into bars. Wrap bars in plastic wrap or bag in snack bags. Bars will stay fresh for one to 2 weeks. Makes 12 to 16 bars.

Chewy Bars

*Julie Jayjohn
Miamisburg, OH*

This is a creamy, chewy, delicious bar. It is a family favorite at every gathering. You cannot stop at just one!

18-1/4 oz. pkg. yellow cake mix	8-oz. pkg. cream cheese, cubed, room temperature
4 eggs, divided	3-1/2 c. powdered sugar
1/2 c. butter, melted	2 t. vanilla extract

In a large bowl, combine dry cake mix, 2 eggs and melted butter; mix well. Batter will be thick. Spread in a greased 13"x9" glass baking pan; pat out evenly with a buttered hand. In a separate bowl, blend cream cheese, powdered sugar, remaining eggs and vanilla. Pour over cake mix layer; spread evenly. Bake at 350 degrees for about 30 minutes, until lightly golden and creamy on top. Cool completely; cut into squares. Makes 2 dozen.

Peg's Oatmeal Cake

Peg Schmeltz
Osceola, IN

My children have always loved this cake and ask me to make it for special occasions like birthdays. It is very much a comfort food.

1 c. rolled oats, uncooked
1-1/2 c. boiling water
1/2 c. margarine
1 c. brown sugar, packed
1 c. sugar

2 eggs, beaten
1 t. vanilla extract
1-1/2 c. all-purpose flour
1 t. cinnamon
1 t. baking soda

Quickly stir oats into boiling water; set aside. In a large bowl, blend together margarine, sugars, eggs and vanilla. Beat well; add flour, cinnamon and baking soda. Stir in oat mixture. Pour batter into a greased 13"x9" baking pan. Bake at 350 degrees for 30 to 35 minutes, until cake tests done with a toothpick. Meanwhile, make Topping. Pour hot topping over hot cake. Place under broiler; broil until bubbly and golden. Makes 15 servings.

Topping:

1 c. sweetened condensed milk
1/2 c. margarine
1 c. brown sugar, packed

1-1/2 c. flaked coconut
Optional: chopped nuts

In a saucepan over medium heat, combine condensed milk, margarine and brown sugar. Bring to a boil. Stir in coconut and nuts, if desired.

If you love to bake, save by purchasing a large bottle of pure vanilla at a club store. Much cheaper than the tiny bottles sold in the supermarket baking aisle!

Applesauce Cake

Caroline Schiller
Bayport, NY

This cake is great for snacking, or add a scoop of ice cream and a drizzle of caramel topping for a yummy dessert.

1/2 c. butter
1 c. sugar
1 egg, beaten
1 t. vanilla extract
1-1/2 c. applesauce
2 c. all-purpose flour
1 t. baking powder

2 t. baking soda
1 t. salt
1 t. cinnamon
1/4 t. ground cloves
Optional: 1 c. raisins,
1 c. chopped nuts

In a large bowl, blend together butter and sugar. Add egg, vanilla and applesauce; mix well and set aside. In a separate bowl, sift together flour, baking powder, baking soda, salt and spices. Add flour mixture to butter mixture; stir well. If desired, fold in raisins and nuts. Pour batter into a greased and floured tube pan. Bake at 350 degrees for 50 minutes. Let cool in pan for several minutes; turn out onto a wire rack and cool completely. Serves 10 to 12.

Charming, yet oh-so-simple...slip a posy-filled mini bud vase into the center of a Bundt cake.

Mom's GO-TO Recipes

Strawberry Dream Cake

Terri Graham
Noblesville, IN

My mom made this special cake for me every birthday, even as an adult. It was the only time of year she made it. It has a wonderfully fresh strawberry flavor.

18-1/2 oz. pkg. white cake mix
3-oz. pkg. strawberry gelatin mix
2 T. all-purpose flour
4 eggs, beaten
1/2 c. water
3/4 c. canola oil, divided
10-oz. pkg. frozen sliced
  strawberries, thawed, juice
  reserved and divided
3 to 4 drops red food coloring

In a large bowl, combine dry mixes, flour, eggs and water. Beat with an electric mixer on medium speed for 2 to 3 minutes. Add half each of oil and strawberries with juice; mix well. Reserve remaining strawberries for icing. Stir in food coloring. Pour batter into 2 greased and floured 8" to 9" round cake pans. Bake at 350 degrees for 35 to 40 minutes, until a toothpick tests done. Assemble and frost cake with Icing. Icing will be thin, but will set up when cake is refrigerated. Serves 12 to 15.

Icing:

1/2 c. butter, softened
16-oz. pkg. powdered sugar
1/2 t. vanilla extract
reserved strawberries with juice
3 to 4 drops red food coloring

In a large bowl, beat butter with an electric mixer on medium speed. Beat in remaining ingredients until smooth.

Frost a layer cake smoothly...no crumbs! Wrap individual layers in plastic wrap and freeze overnight. The next day, unwrap layers and frost right away, while still frozen. The cake will still be firm, so frosting is easier to spread.

Mom's Best DESSERTS

Cherry-Walnut Crisp

Lori Simmons
Princeville, IL

This scrumptious dessert is easy to make and good with any fruit pie filling you like. Apricot is especially good.

21-oz. can cherry pie filling
1/4 c. all-purpose flour
1/4 c. quick-cooking oats,
    uncooked
1/4 c. brown sugar, packed

3/4 t. cinnamon
1/4 c. chopped walnuts
2 T. butter
Garnish: ice cream or
    whipped topping

Spread pie filling in a lightly greased 8"x8" baking pan; set aside. In a large bowl, mix flour, oats, brown sugar, cinnamon and walnuts. Cut in butter with 2 forks until mixture is crumbly; sprinkle over pie filling. Bake at 400 degrees for 25 minutes, or until bubbly and golden. Serve warm with a scoop of ice cream or whipped topping. Makes 6 servings.

Top off your best desserts with fresh whipped cream. With an electric mixer on high speed, beat one cup heavy cream until soft peaks form. Add one tablespoon sugar and one teaspoon vanilla extract, then continue to beat until stiff peaks form. Scrumptious!

Ɱ☐m's GO-TO Recipes

Mom's Cowboy Cookies

Marsha Baker
Pioneer, OH

This is my brothers' and my favorite cookie. Our mom was quite a cookie baker, sometimes spending a whole day baking all kinds of cookies for the freezer, for school lunches and for drop-in company. This is the cookie we all still talk about many years later.

1 c. butter, softened
1 c. brown sugar, packed
1 c. sugar
2 eggs, beaten
2 c. all-purpose flour
1/2 t. baking powder
1 t. baking soda

1/2 t. salt
2 c. rolled oats, uncooked
1 t. vanilla extract
12-oz. pkg. semi-sweet
   chocolate chips
Optional: 1/2 c. chopped nuts

In a large bowl, blend butter and sugars until smooth; add eggs and beat until light and fluffy. Add flour, baking powder, baking soda and salt; mix well. Add oats and vanilla; stir in chocolate chips and nuts, if using. Drop dough by tablespoonfuls onto ungreased baking sheets, 2 inches apart. Bake at 350 degrees for 12 minutes, or until golden. Makes about 8 dozen.

Serve up warm, fresh-baked cookies anytime. Roll your favorite cookie dough into balls and freeze them on a tray, then pop them into a freezer bag. Later, just pull out the number of cookies you need, thaw briefly and bake.

Peanut Butter & Jelly Bars

Lori Simmons
Princeville, IL

If your kids like peanut butter & jelly sandwiches, they will surely love these cookie bars! Kids especially like grape jelly and strawberry jam, but you can use any flavor.

16-1/2 oz. tube refrigerated
   peanut butter cookie dough
1/2 c. peanut butter chips

16-oz. can buttercream frosting
1/4 c. creamy peanut butter
1/4 c. favorite jam or jelly

Let dough soften for 5 to 10 minutes at room temperature. Press dough into an ungreased 13"x9" baking pan; sprinkle with peanut butter chips. Bake at 375 degrees for 15 to 18 minutes, until lightly golden and edges are firm to the touch. Remove from oven. In a small bowl, beat together frosting and peanut butter until smooth. Spread over bars. Drop jam over frosting by teaspoonfuls. Cut through frosting with a table knife to swirl jam. Cut into bars. Makes 2 dozen.

Once in a young lifetime, one should be allowed to have as much sweetness as one can possibly want and hold.

– Judith Olney

Mom's GO-TO *Recipes*

Cocoa Crazy Cake

Barbara Severin
Winner, SD

I have no idea how many of these cakes I've made over the years!
I have been making this cake since I was 11 or 12, and I am going on
80 years! Everyone in my family, and good friends too, wants this
chocolate cake with its delicious icing for birthdays and more.

3 c. sugar
3 c. all-purpose flour
1/3 c. baking cocoa
2 t. baking soda
Optional: 1 t. salt

2 t. vinegar
1 t. vanilla extract
3/4 c. oil
2 c. water

In a large bowl, combine all ingredients; mix well. Pour batter into a
greased 13"x9" baking pan. Bake at 350 degrees for 50 minutes. About
15 minutes before cake is done, start making Luscious Peanut Butter
Icing. Remove cake from oven; immediately pour hot icing over hot
cake. Cool. Makes 12 to 15 servings.

Luscious Peanut Butter Icing:

2 c. brown sugar, packed
1/2 c. milk
1-1/2 t. vanilla extract

2 t. margarine
1/3 c. creamy peanut butter

In a saucepan over medium heat, combine brown sugar and milk; bring
to a boil. Reduce heat slightly; boil for 5 minutes. Remove from heat.
Add vanilla, margarine and peanut butter; stir until fairly thick.

A little coffee brings out the flavor in
chocolate desserts. Dissolve a tablespoon
of instant coffee granules in the liquid
ingredients and continue as directed.

Mom's Best DESSERTS

Pecan Crunch Ice Cream Dessert

Sue Klapper
Muskego, WI

This is the best ice cream dessert ever! I've made this awesome dessert at least once every summer for over 30 years, ever since my friend first served it at a party. It can feed a crowd of very happy people!

1/2 c. brown sugar, packed	1 c. butter, melted
2 c. all-purpose flour	12-oz. jar favorite ice cream
1 c. chopped pecans	topping, divided
1 c. quick-cooking oats,	1/2 gal. favorite ice cream
uncooked	

In a bowl, mix all ingredients except ice cream topping and ice cream. Spread on a lightly greased 15"x10" jelly-roll pan. Bake at 400 degrees for 10 minutes; stir. Bake for another 5 minutes, or until golden. Cool; crumble half of mixture into an ungreased 13"x9" glass baking pan. Spoon half of ice cream topping over crumb mixture. Slice ice cream and arrange slices over topping. Crumble remaining crumb mixture on top; drizzle with remaining topping. Cover and freeze. Soften slightly before serving. Makes 18 servings.

Cake doughnuts make yummy ice cream sandwiches. Cut a doughnut in half and add a scoop of softened ice cream between the 2 halves. Set on a baking sheet and freeze for one hour...tasty!

Mom's GO-TO *Recipes*

Dutch Crunch Apple-Walnut Bars *Lori Ritchey*
Denver, PA

*Great for an after-school snack, or serve warm with
vanilla ice cream for a yummy dessert.*

2 c. all-purpose flour
1 t. baking soda
1/4 t. salt
1 t. cinnamon
1/2 t. nutmeg
1 c. unsweetened smooth or
  chunky applesauce

1 c. sugar
1 t. vanilla extract
1/2 c. chopped walnuts
2 T. butter, softened
1/4 c. brown sugar, packed
2/3 c. corn flake cereal, crushed

In a bowl, combine flour, baking soda, salt and spices; mix well and set aside. In a large bowl, beat together applesauce, sugar and vanilla. Gradually blend flour mixture into applesauce mixture; stir in walnuts. Spread mixture evenly in a lightly greased 13"x9" baking pan; set aside. In a small bowl, blend butter and brown sugar; gradually blend in cereal. Spread over dough. Bake at 350 degrees for 30 minutes, or until lightly golden. Cool in pan; cut into large or small bars. Makes one to 2 dozen.

For perfectly cut brownies or bars, refrigerate them in the pan
for about an hour after baking. Cut them with a plastic
knife for a clean cut every time.

Mom's Best DESSERTS

German Chocolate Cake Cookies

Betty Lou Wright
Fort Worth, TX

These have become my family's newest favorite cookies. Loaded with chocolate chips to enhance the mild German chocolate flavor, they are soft and chewy. A hint of cinnamon makes chocolate even better. These freeze well.

18-1/2 oz. pkg. German chocolate cake mix	1 t. vanilla extract
1/2 c. butter, softened	1/8 to 1/4 t. cinnamon
2 eggs, beaten	1 c. milk chocolate chips
2 T. oil	1/2 c. semi-sweet chocolate chips
	3/4 c. sweetened flaked coconut

In a large bowl, combine dry cake mix, butter, eggs and oil. Beat with an electric mixer on medium speed for 2 minutes. Stir in vanilla and cinnamon; fold in chocolate chips and coconut. Drop batter by rounded teaspoonfuls onto parchment paper-lined baking sheets. Bake at 350 degrees for 12 to 13 minutes. Cool cookies on baking sheets for 3 minutes; transfer to wire racks and cool. Store in an airtight container. Makes 3 dozen.

Deliver a tray of your favorite goodies to the teachers' lounge at school...it's sure to be appreciated!

Mom's GO-TO Recipes

Diana's Carrot Sheet Cake

Marian Forck
Chamois, MO

My friend used to make this cake and bring it to work to share. Everyone just had to have a piece! Since it's baked in a jelly-roll pan, there's plenty for everybody. It is the best carrot cake I have ever tasted...it will become your favorite too. You will totally enjoy this cake!

2 c. sugar
1-1/2 c. oil
4 eggs, well beaten
2 c. all-purpose flour
2 t. baking powder
2 t. baking soda

1 t. salt
2 t. cinnamon
1 t. vanilla extract
3 c. carrots, peeled and finely
   grated
1/2 c. chopped pecans

In a large bowl, beat sugar and oil with an electric mixer on medium speed; add eggs and mix well. Add flour, baking powder, baking soda, salt and cinnamon; beat until mixed. Stir in vanilla; fold in carrots and pecans. Pour into a greased 15"x10" jelly-roll pan. Bake at 300 degrees oven for 40 to 50 minutes, until a toothpick inserted in the center comes out clean. Cool; spread Cream Cheese Icing over cake. Refrigerate until ready to serve. Makes 30 to 35 servings.

Cream Cheese Icing:

8-oz. pkg. cream cheese,
   softened
1/4 c. butter, softened

16-oz. pkg. powdered sugar
2 t. vanilla extract

In a large bowl, beat cream cheese and butter until blended. Beat in powdered sugar until smooth and spreadable; stir in vanilla.

Better with butter! For the most delicious baked goods,
use only real butter, not margarine.

Mom's Best DESSERTS

Apple Crisp Muffins

Mel Chencharick
Julian, PA

This recipe reminds me of the McIntosh muffins we had when I was younger. A great-tasting muffin!

3-1/2 c. all-purpose flour
2 c. sugar
1 t. baking soda
1 t. salt
1 t. cinnamon
1-1/4 c. oil

2 eggs, lightly beaten
1 t. vanilla extract
3 c. apples, peeled, cored
    and diced
Optional: 1/2 c. chopped pecans

In a large bowl, combine flour, sugar, baking soda, salt and cinnamon. Stir in oil, eggs and vanilla; fold in apples and pecans, if using. Spoon batter into 24 greased or paper-lined muffin cups, filling to just below the rim. Bake at 350 degrees for 30 minutes, or until a toothpick inserted in the center tests clean. Cool muffins in pan on a wire rack for 5 minutes before removing from pan. Makes 2 dozen.

Fruit muffins make yummy mini "sandwiches." Just slice in half and spread with softened cream cheese...a great lunchtime or after-school snack!

Mom's GO-TO Recipes

Chocolate Oatmeal Pie

Delores Lakes
Mansfield, OH

*This is truly a comfort dessert from the past, and is still oh-so good!
My husband loves it, served with a little vanilla bean ice cream
on top. It is delicious served alone, too.*

9" pie crust, unbaked
1/3 c. semi-sweet chocolate chips
1/3 c. butter, melted
2/3 c. sugar
1 c. light or dark corn syrup

3 eggs, beaten
1 T. vanilla extract
1-1/4 c. old-fashioned oats,
   uncooked
Optional: vanilla ice cream

Press pie crust into a 9" pie plate. Scatter chocolate chips evenly over
crust; set aside. In a large bowl, mix butter and sugar until smooth and
creamy. Whisk in corn syrup, eggs and vanilla until well blended. Fold
in oats. Pour batter over chocolate chips in crust. Bake at 350 degrees
for 45 minutes, or until a knife tip inserted in the center comes out
clean. Set pan on a wire rack to cool. Top with a scoop of ice cream,
if desired. Makes 8 servings.

Carrying a pie to a potluck or party? A bamboo steamer from
an import store is just the thing...it can even hold 2 pies at once.

Mom's Best
DESSERTS

Frozen Peanut Butter Pie

Rachel Harter
The Woodlands, TX

*My Gran used to make this creamy pie all the time when I was
growing up. It was my Pawpaw's favorite, and now it is
a must for family gatherings!*

1/2 c. creamy peanut butter
1/2 c. cream cheese, softened
1 c. powdered sugar
1/2 c. milk

8-oz. container frozen whipped
  topping, thawed
9-inch vanilla wafer or chocolate
  cookie crust

In a large bowl, blend together peanut butter, cream cheese, powdered
sugar and milk. Fold whipped topping into peanut butter mixture. Spoon
into crust; cover and freeze for at least 4 hours. At serving time, let
stand at room temperature for about 5 minutes to make slicing easy.
Makes 8 servings.

Go-To Brownies

Gwen Gooda
Manitoba, Canada

*This is my tried & true recipe for brownies in a hurry. I used to
make them for the guys at work when I worked weekends
and they were always a hit!*

2 eggs
18-1/2 oz. pkg. chocolate
  cake mix
1/2 c. butter, melted and cooled
  slightly

12-oz. pkg. semi-sweet
  chocolate chips
1 c. pecan pieces
Garnish: powdered sugar

Beat eggs in a large bowl. Add dry cake mix and butter; mix well to
form a stiff batter. Fold in chocolate chips and pecans; mix well. Spray a
13"x9" baking pan with non-stick vegetable spray; line with wax paper.
Spread batter in pan. Bake at 350 degrees for 18 to 20 minutes; do not
overbake. Cool completely; lift brownies out of pan with wax paper
edges. Sprinkle generously with powdered sugar; cut into bars. Makes
one dozen.

Mom's GO-TO Recipes

Chocolate Chip Skillet Cookies

Tina Butler
Royse City, TX

"Baking and Game Night" is is a tradition in our family! We bake a sweet treat together as a family and then enjoy it while we play a favorite board game. This is a special favorite in our house. Serve it plain or top with a scoop of ice cream...yum!

2-1/4 c. all-purpose flour	1 t. vanilla extract
1 t. baking soda	2 eggs, beaten
1/2 t. salt	12-oz. pkg. semi-sweet
1 c. butter, softened	chocolate chips
3/4 c. light brown sugar, packed	Optional: 1 c. chopped nuts
3/4 c. sugar	Garnish: vanilla ice cream

In a bowl, stir together flour, baking soda and salt; set aside. In a separate large bowl, beat butter, sugars and vanilla with an electric mixer on medium speed until creamy. Add eggs; beat well. Gradually add flour mixture, beating well. With a spoon, fold in chocolate chips and nuts, if desired. Press dough into a large oven-proof skillet. Press to flatten, covering the bottom of pan. Bake at 375 degrees for 40 to 45 minutes, until golden. If cookie starts to brown too quickly, cover with aluminum foil sprayed with a bit of non-stick vegetable spray and continue baking. Transfer pan to a wire rack to cool, 15 to 20 minutes. To serve, cut into wedges; top each with a scoop of ice cream. Makes 8 servings.

Take time to share an icy glass of milk and a favorite treat
with the kids after school...it's a great way to
catch up and make sweet memories.

Mom's Best DESSERTS

Easy Apple Tart

Sandra Monroe
Preston, MD

This is so easy to make...often requested in our home! Top with cinnamon ice cream for an extra-special treat.

6 Granny Smith apples, peeled, cored and thinly sliced
2 T. lemon juice
1/4 c. sugar
1/3 c. brown sugar, packed
1/2 c. all-purpose flour
1/2 t. cinnamon
3 T. butter
9-inch pie crust, unbaked
Garnish: ice cream

In a bowl, toss together apples, lemon juice and sugar; set aside. In a large bowl, mix together brown sugar, flour and cinnamon. Cut in butter until mixture is crumbly and set aside. On a floured surface, roll pie crust into a 13-inch circle; place on a pizza baking pan. Gently mound apples in center of crust, leaving a 2-inch border of crust on all sides. Sprinkle apples with brown sugar mixture. Fold crust over filling, pleating sides as necessary to fit snugly around apples. Gently press crust into filling, reinforcing the shape. Bake at 400 degrees for about 30 minutes, until crust is golden and apples are tender. Set pan on a wire rack and cool for 10 minutes. Serve warm with a scoop of ice cream. Makes 4 to 6 servings.

Create a heavenly glaze for any apple dessert. Melt together 1/2 cup butterscotch chips, 2 tablespoons butter and 2 tablespoons whipping cream over low heat. Stir until smooth.

Mom's GO-TO *Recipes*

Frosted Lemon Sheet Cake

Carol Miller
Gordon, TX

*We made this for a Ladies' Day at church. It was a big hit
and several ladies asked for the recipe.*

18-1/2 oz. pkg. lemon cake mix
4 eggs, beaten
zest of 1 lemon

15-3/4 oz. can lemon pie filling
Optional: thin lemon slices

In a large bowl, beat dry cake mix and eggs with an electric mixer on medium speed until well blended. Stir in lemon zest; fold in pie filling. Spread batter in a greased 15"x10" jelly-roll pan. Bake at 350 degrees for 18 to 20 minutes, until a toothpick inserted near the center comes out clean. Set pan on a wire rack; cool. Spread cooled cake with Frosting. Garnish squares of cake with lemon slices, if desired. Makes 20 to 30 servings.

Frosting:

3-oz. pkg. cream cheese,
    softened
1/2 c. butter, softened

juice of 1 lemon
2 to 2-1/2 c. powered sugar

In a bowl, beat cream cheese, butter, lemon juice and powdered sugar until smooth. Beat in enough powdered sugar to make a spreadable consistency.

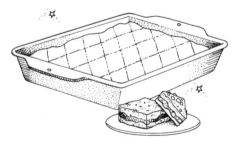

Serving cake to a crowd? A 15"x10" jelly-roll pan is your best choice. Cut it into as many small pieces as you need... up to 60, if each piece is 1-3/4 by 1-1/2 inches. After a big dinner, this will be plenty for dessert.

Mom's Best DESSERTS

Fluffy Fruit Dessert

Mildred Gochenour
Harrisonburg, VA

At a potluck, I enjoyed sampling a dessert similar to this. I've experimented with different fruits and methods to perfect this recipe. It gets rave reviews...no one can believe it's so easy to make! The recipe may be doubled using a 13"x9" glass baking pan.

8-oz. container frozen whipped topping, thawed
3-oz. pkg. peach gelatin mix
6-oz. container peach yogurt
1-1/2 c. peaches, peeled, pitted and chopped

2 sleeves graham crackers
Optional: additional sliced peaches

In a large bowl, combine whipped topping and dry gelatin mix; mix well. Stir in yogurt; fold in peaches and set aside. Arrange whole graham crackers in the bottom of an ungreased 10"x8" glass baking pan. Spread peach mixture evenly over graham crackers. Crush remaining graham crackers and sprinkle over top. Garnish top with additional sliced peaches, if desired. Cover and refrigerate several hours before serving. Makes 8 servings.

Variations:

• Lighten it up: use light whipped topping and sugar-free gelatin mix for a lower calorie, low-fat dessert.

• Swap out the fruit flavor: for example, chopped strawberries, strawberry gelatin mix and strawberry yogurt. Raspberries are good too.

• Make a delicious frozen pie: spoon fruit mixture into a graham cracker crust and freeze.

A sprinkle of finely crushed graham crackers is an easy garnish for any pie in a crumb crust.

Mom's GO-TO *Recipes*

Mary's Pantry Cookies

Mary Warren
Sanford, MI

My family loves these cookies! I began with a very basic cookie recipe and over the years I've added and subtracted various items. The recipe is very forgiving, so add what you have in the pantry. Dried cranberries, raisins and white chocolate chips are all good.

1 c. shortening
1 c. brown sugar, packed
1 c. sugar
1 t. vanilla extract
2 eggs
2 c. all-purpose flour
1/2 t. baking powder
1 t. baking soda

1/2 t. salt
1-1/2 c. old-fashioned oats, uncooked
2 c. crispy rice cereal
1 c. flaked coconut
1/2 c. mini semi-sweet chocolate chips

In a large bowl, blend shortening, sugars and vanilla. Beat in eggs, one at a time; set aside. In a separate bowl, mix flour, baking powder, baking soda and salt; add to shortening mixture and stir well. Fold in remaining ingredients. Scoop dough into balls by tablespoonfuls; place on ungreased baking sheets. Press down slightly, using the palm of your hand. Bake at 350 degrees for 11 to 14 minutes. Makes about 4 dozen.

Not sure if the can of baking powder in the cupboard is still good? Try this simple test...stir one teaspoon baking powder into 1/2 cup hot water. If it fizzes, go ahead and use it...if not, toss it out. To check baking soda, add 1/4 teaspoon baking soda to 2 teaspoons of vinegar. It should fizz up.

Mom's Best
DESSERTS

Grandma Cora's Butterballs

Leona Krivda
Belle Vernon, PA

I remember my Grandma Cora always making these cookies. My mom made them and now I do too...I'm sure my daughters and granddaughter will add them to their cookie list also! Roll them in beaten egg white and tinted coconut before baking, if you like.

1 c. butter
1/4 c. powdered sugar
2 t. vanilla extract
1 T. water

2 c. all-purpose flour
1 c. chopped walnuts
Garnish: powdered sugar

In a bowl, beat butter, sugar and vanilla well, until light and fluffy. Stir in water and flour; mix well. Fold in nuts. Shape dough into 1-1/4 inch balls; roll in powdered sugar. Place on ungreased baking sheets. Bake at 300 degrees for 18 to 20 minutes. Makes 2 dozen.

Easy Butterscotch Cookies

Janelle Johnson
Clayton, WI

Grandma made these goodies every year for Christmas, and now that she's gone, I continue to make them. They are one of my favorites and very easy to make.

12-oz. pkg. butterscotch chips
1/4 c. creamy peanut butter

4 c. corn flake cereal
1 c. salted peanuts

Melt butterscotch chips and peanut butter in a double boiler over medium heat, cooking only until melted. Remove from heat; stir until smooth. Add corn flakes and peanuts; stir carefully until coated. Drop by tablespoonfuls onto wax paper. Let stand until firm. Makes 3 to 4 dozen.

The best way to make children good
is to make them happy.

– Oscar Wilde

Mom's GO-TO *Recipes*

Light-as-a-Cloud Cheesecake

Denise Webb
Newington, GA

This is the cake my mom always made when I was growing up. It is delicious and light, especially topped with strawberry syrup or fresh raspberries.

3-oz. pkg. lemon gelatin mix
1 c. boiling water
8-oz. pkg. cream cheese,
  softened

1 c. sugar
1 t. vanilla extract
12-oz. can evaporated milk,
  chilled

Make Graham Cracker Crust; set aside. Dissolve gelatin mix in boiling water; let stand to room temperature, until set. Meanwhile, in a separate bowl, beat cream cheese until softened. Beat in sugar and vanilla; set aside. Pour chilled milk into another bowl; beat with an electric mixer on medium-high speed until soft peaks form. Fold gelatin mixture into whipped milk. Add to cream cheese mixture; mix gently. Spoon into graham cracker crust; cover and chill. Makes 15 to 20 servings.

Graham Cracker Crust:

2 sleeves graham crackers,
  crushed

1/2 c. sugar
3/4 c. butter, softened

Combine graham cracker crumbs, sugar and butter. Press into a 13"x9" baking pan; chill.

For crumb crusts, instead of graham crackers try vanilla wafers, gingersnaps or even pretzels, for a yummy sweet & salty taste.

Mom's Best **DESSERTS**

Poor Man's Cobbler

Andrea Gast
O'Fallon, MO

My mom, Georgetta D'Angelo, has been baking this recipe for our family since I was a small girl. It smells heavenly while it's baking. I remember it being served piping-hot from the oven with a scoop of ice cream on top...yum!

1-1/2 c. butter
1 c. all-purpose flour
1 c. sugar
1 t. baking powder
1/4 t. salt

3/4 c. milk
15-oz. can sliced peaches
    or sweet cherries
Garnish: vanilla ice cream

Melt butter in a 12"x10" baking pan; spread to coat pan and set aside. In a bowl, combine flour, sugar, baking powder, salt and milk; stir well. Pour batter over butter in pan. Spoon fruit and its juice gently over batter; do not mix. Bake at 350 degrees for one hour, or until bubbly and golden. Serve warm, topped with a scoop of ice cream. Makes 10 servings.

Whip up some homemade cherry pie filling in no time. Combine one pound pitted tart cherries, 3/4 cup sugar, 1/3 cup cornstarch and 2 tablespoons lemon juice in a saucepan over medium heat. Bring to a boil, then simmer until thickened...yummy!

Anytime Pumpkin Bars

Linda Potter
Freedom, PA

This recipe is a favorite with my family. The bars freeze well, so I always have some in the freezer for unexpected guests.

2 c. canned pumpkin	1 t. baking soda
1 c. applesauce or oil	1 t. salt
4 eggs, well beaten	2 t. cinnamon
1 t. vanilla extract	1 t. ground ginger
2 c. all-purpose flour	1 c. chopped nuts
2 c. sugar	3/4 c. raisins

In a large bowl, whisk together pumpkin, applesauce or oil, eggs and vanilla; set aside. In a separate bowl, combine flour, sugar, baking soda, salt and spices; mix well. Stir flour mixture into pumpkin mixture; fold in nuts and raisins. Pour batter into a greased 13"x9" baking pan. Bake at 350 degrees for 30 to 35 minutes, until a knife tip inserted in the center comes out clean. Cool; cut into bars. Makes 3 dozen.

For an easy-to-make frosting that's not too sweet, simply blend together a 16-ounce can of prepared frosting with an 8-ounce package of softened cream cheese.

Mom's Best DESSERTS

Gooey Butter Cookies

Dawn Thompson
Saint Charles, MO

Saint Louis lays claim to being the home of the gooey butter coffee cake. These cookies are an easy way to enjoy this treat. Whenever I make them for my family, they disappear quickly!

1/2 c. butter, softened
8-oz. pkg. cream cheese,
  softened
1 egg, beaten

1/4 t. vanilla extract
18-1/2 oz. pkg. butter recipe
  yellow cake mix
1/2 c. powdered sugar

In a large bowl, combine butter, cream cheese, egg and vanilla; beat together until fluffy. Stir in dry cake mix; cover and chill for 30 minutes. Drop dough by teaspoonfuls into powdered sugar; roll into balls. Place on ungreased baking sheets. Bake at 350 degrees for 10 to 13 minutes. Makes 2 dozen.

Devil's Food Cake Mix Cookies

Irene Robinson
Cincinnati, OH

With this recipe, you can make lots of cookies in a jiffy! Works great with other flavors of cake mix too.

18-1/2 oz. pkg. devil's food
  cake mix
8-oz. container frozen whipped
  topping, thawed

1 egg, lightly beaten
Optional: 1 c. chopped pecans
1/2 c. powdered sugar

In a large bowl, combine dry cake mix, topping and egg; stir well. Dough will be sticky. Stir in pecans, if desired. Dust hands with powdered sugar; shape dough into 3/4-inch balls. Coat balls with powdered sugar; place on ungreased baking sheets, 2 inches apart. Bake at 350 degrees for 10 to 12 minutes. Remove to wire racks to cool. Makes 5 dozen.

Add color to a cookie tray. Simply stir in some colored sugar before rolling balls of drop cookie dough in sugar.

217

INDEX

INDEX

INDEX

Find Gooseberry Patch
wherever you are!

www.gooseberrypatch.com

Call us toll-free at 1·800·854·6673

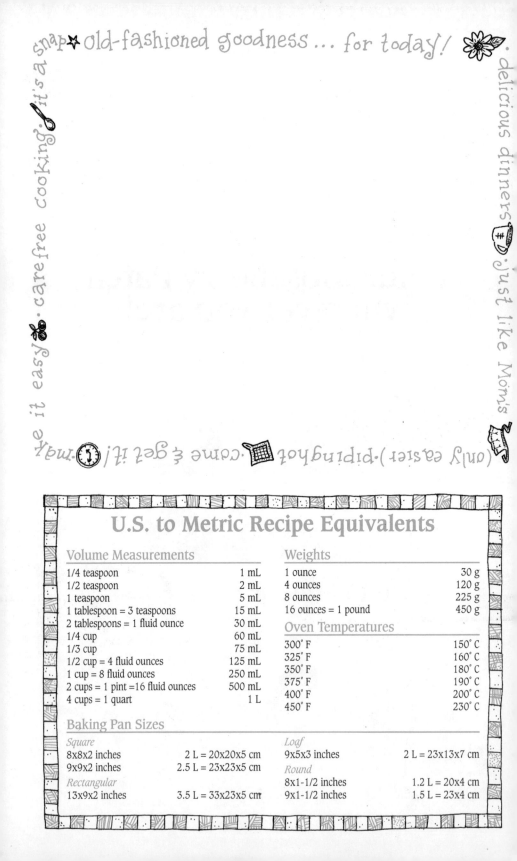

old-fashioned goodness ... for today!

delicious dinners · just like Mom's · (only easier) · piping hot · come & get it! · make it easy · carefree cooking · it's a snap

U.S. to Metric Recipe Equivalents

Volume Measurements

1/4 teaspoon	1 mL
1/2 teaspoon	2 mL
1 teaspoon	5 mL
1 tablespoon = 3 teaspoons	15 mL
2 tablespoons = 1 fluid ounce	30 mL
1/4 cup	60 mL
1/3 cup	75 mL
1/2 cup = 4 fluid ounces	125 mL
1 cup = 8 fluid ounces	250 mL
2 cups = 1 pint =16 fluid ounces	500 mL
4 cups = 1 quart	1 L

Weights

1 ounce	30 g
4 ounces	120 g
8 ounces	225 g
16 ounces = 1 pound	450 g

Oven Temperatures

300° F	150° C
325° F	160° C
350° F	180° C
375° F	190° C
400° F	200° C
450° F	230° C

Baking Pan Sizes

Square

8x8x2 inches	2 L = 20x20x5 cm
9x9x2 inches	2.5 L = 23x23x5 cm

Rectangular

13x9x2 inches	3.5 L = 33x23x5 cm

Loaf

9x5x3 inches	2 L = 23x13x7 cm

Round

8x1-1/2 inches	1.2 L = 20x4 cm
9x1-1/2 inches	1.5 L = 23x4 cm